THE
PIMM'S BOOK OF
POLO

THE SPLENDOUR OF THE QUEEN'S HOUSEHOLD CAVALRY AT THE
GUARDS POLO CLUB, WINDSOR GREAT PARK.

THE
PIMM'S BOOK OF
POLO

MAJOR RONALD FERGUSON
EDITORIAL ADVISER

JOHN LLOYD
WITH
MICHAEL ROBERTS

Trafalgar Square Publishing
NORTH POMFRET, VERMONT

PIMM'S AND LEMONADE

1 x Pimm's

2 x Lemonade, 7-Up or Ginger Ale

Plenty of ice

Decorate with a slice of lemon,
or orange and cucumber if desired

PIMM'S SEVILLA

Frost glass with sugar

1 x Pimm's

2 x fresh orange juice

Plenty of ice

Decorate with a slice of lemon

VROOM!

1 x Pimm's

1 x Tequila, Vodka or Gin

3 x Lemonade, 7-Up or Ginger Ale

Plenty of ice

Decorate with a slice of lemon,
and sprig of fresh mint

PIMM'S ROYAL

1 x Pimm's

2 x Demi Sec Champagne or
semi sweet sparkling wine

Plenty of ice

Decorate with a slice of orange

Original Concept, Research and Design by Terry Allen

With special thanks to the following contributors:
H.H. The Rajmata of Jaipur, Dr. Vik Advani, Major Hugh Dawnay
Major R. I. Ferguson, Lady Edith Foxwell, David and Janette Lominska
John Lloyd, Major Willy Loyd, Bryan Morrison
Ronald Mullings, Major Jack Pringle, Michael Roberts
Frank Rohr, Jack and Marjorie Williams

© *Mackenzie Publishing Limited* 178 Royal College Street, London NW1 0PS, Great Britain

Publisher: **Terry Allen**,　Design Assistant: **Christine Nys**
Editor: **Jeff Groman**,　Project Co-ordinator: **Christina Grant**

First published in the United States of America
in 1989 by
Trafalgar Square Publishing, North Pomfret,
Vermont 05053.

ISBN: 0 94395 17 3

LOC : 89-50098

Colour origination by Brian Gregory Associates Ltd
Typesetting by Tameside Filmsetting Ltd and Keene Graphics Ltd, London
Printed and bound by Royal Smeets Offset, BV, Netherlands

CONTENTS

FOREWORD

I FEEL VERY FORTUNATE to have been able to play polo all over the world for thirty-four years. During this time it has been my privilege to meet many warm and generous polo supporters. Polo is the most international of games and for sheer thrills and excitement I don't believe the game can be equalled. We can all unite in appreciating the joy of man and horse in perfect harmony, working together for the good of their team.

Now, whilst in the twilight of my polo life I am dedicated to give as much back to the game as I have taken out of it.

I have been involved with Pimm's for many years and it gives me very great pleasure to be involved with The Pimm's Book of Polo. Some years ago I played for a team sponsored by Pimm's. Then as now it seemed fitting that this splendid drink should be seen to be playing its part in the game. What could be better for player or spectator alike than to enjoy a refreshing glass of Pimm's after a match?

John Lloyd has been writing about polo for many years, recording it both as a sport and a social phenomenon so he is well qualified to produce this celebration of the game which we love so much. He has observed the sport all over the world, from its cradle in India to some of the youngest clubs in the United States of America. He has written this book with the support of three foremost polo writers, Major William Loyd, Major Hugh Dawnay and Frank Rohr. The book is magnificently presented with superb photography.

In 1988 the Museum of Polo and Hall of Fame was inaugurated in Lexington, Kentucky. This commemorates the sport, houses some of its art and memorabilia and honours those who have played influential parts in polo's history. Perhaps in its own way The Pimm's Book of Polo does the same. Certainly it comes at the right time, for 1990 marks the one hundredth anniversary of the setting up of the United States Polo Association; an occasion which surely deserves much celebration.

I am pleased to be able to acknowledge the support that Pimm's give to the game. I recommend this book to you. I am sure it will provide many hours of pleasure and, I hope, encourage you to play or watch polo all over the world.

R I Ferguson

مرکب بجانب اورا راند چون دید که بزدیک وی غنم آمدن
دار درد بگر بیت و کفت بیت انگس که مراگشت بازامدش
تا که دلش سوخت برگشته خویش چنانکه ملاطفت کرد و پرسید

کجو نی و از کجای چه صنعت دانی در تفریح جر محبت و مودت
جان عزیزی مانده که مجال نفس زدن نذاشت بیت
اگر خود لطفت سبع از بر جوانی چو آشفتی الف بی تی ندانی

TO THE RULERS OF THE PERSIAN EMPIRE, POLO WAS
RANKED NEXT TO BATTLE ITSELF AS THE ULTIMATE TEST OF THE
PROWESS OF PRINCES AND WARRIORS

1

THE FIRST 2000 YEARS

Where the game of polo was born will never be known – but written accounts tell of it being played by Iranian tribesmen some 600 years before the birth of Christ. What is known, however, is that when Lieutenant Joseph Sherer – dubbed "The Father of English Polo" in Calcutta in 1864 and who must be credited with the spread of the modern game – first came across it being played by local tribesmen at Silchar in the northeastern Indian state of Manipur, he is said to have become excited and exclaimed "we must learn this game!"

The local ruler, though pleased, felt constrained to point out that his people had been playing the sport for more than 2,000 years. The Manipuris called their game by two names, *kán-jāi-bazèè* and *pulu*, and it was the latter, referring to the wooden ball which was used, that over the centuries was taken up by the sport in its slow spread to the West.

Although the ancient origins of the game are obscure, there is a clue, perhaps, in the present-day primitive versions of it played as far apart as Japan, Russia and Turkey. Fierce mounted mêlées test the horsemanship and courage of the participants of such games as *da-kyu* (spoon polo) in Japan, *khis-kouhou*, the bridal chase of the Russian steppes, and *djerid*, the warlike javelin game of Turkey.

A rough form of polo is played in an annual tournament at Gilgat in northern Pakistan. In this extreme test of bravery and horsemanship deaths are frequently recorded on the long, narrow playing field bordered by low stone walls. Each period of play lasts for 30 minutes and no substitute of man or pony is allowed. The tradition of the game in this place is a proud one and the tournament programme states: "The game of polo was born in Central Asia, spent its childhood in Iran and attained maturity in the northern areas."

The first great Persian Empire under Darius I (550–486 BC) took its culture to Egypt, Greece and northern India. The horse played its considerable part in this proliferation and it is likely that the game of *chaugán*, as polo was then known, was enjoyed by the court and the cavalry in its newly-won territories. Thus, much as the name of the modern game is derived from the native word for a ball, so the early version was called after the mallet or stick used.

Some authorities believe that the game originated in Tibet, where legend has it that an annual gathering took place in the autumn to hunt the muskrat. The animal was chased on horseback and when finally captured beaten to death with a stick carried for the purpose. For practice in the summer – when no rats were to be found – the riders used a root ball covered with animal skin.

Despite the Tibetan factor, a Persian origin for the game seems most likely, in view of the supremacy of that historical people and their known equestrian abilities. Certainly later historians had no doubt that the game was well established by the time of Alexander the Great of Macedonia in the fourth century BC. When this fine cavalry officer took over from his father in 336 BC, it is said that the Emperor of Persia, Darius III Codomannos, sent him a polo stick and ball with the message that he should continue with such sports and leave warmongering alone. Made of sterner stuff, the young Alexander thanked him for the gifts and replied that for him they were purely symbolic. He was the stick and the ball represented the earth which he intended to conquer. If he excelled at polo as at everything else – for he soon defeated Darius – then Alexander must have been an early high-goal player.

As empires spread so did the game and it is recorded as being played throughout Asia Minor, China and the Indian subcontinent. Persians, Arabs, the Chinese and the Moguls all enjoyed polo and it is clear that besides providing exciting recreation for the ruling classes, both men and women, it was also used as a means of encouraging necessary good horsemanship amongst the warrior class. Not only could they improve their skills but it represented a severe test of courage – qualities highly regarded for those ambitious for political and military power.

THE GAME AS PLAYED IN GILGAT IN MODERN-DAY PAKISTAN PERHAPS REPRESENTS MOST NEARLY POLO AS IT HAS BEEN PLAYED IN THE PAST.

THE GAME WAS WELL ESTABLISHED WHEN THIS EIGHTH CENTURY
T'ANG DYNASTY POTTERY LADY POLO PLAYER WAS CRAFTED.

The ancient game would hardly be recognised by its modern exponents. At times it involved as many as 200 players and must have appeared like a miniature battle. However, in its more courtly mode it was a gentler sport and by the time it began to be recorded by historians it had already taken on a more recognisable form.

Dinvari, the ninth-century Persian astronomer and historian, offered general rules for the game which included the avoidance of strong language and an attempt at patience. Other, more poetic, writings speak eloquently of the game, capturing even then the beauty and excitement which was to thrill and enthuse all who have enjoyed polo up to the present time. Polo was used to illustrate his philosophical points by Omar Khayyām in his eleventh-century verses, and many others after him found it a useful vehicle for the making of moral points. For instance, the Persian poet Nizāmī gave advice on how to live a full life: "The horizon is the edge of your polo field, the earth is the ball in the curve of your polo stick. Until you are blotted out of existence as the dust, gallop and press on your horse for the ground is yours."

The importance of the sport can be deduced from the appearance of a polo stick on Chinese royal coats of arms and T'ang dynasty tomb figures of the seventh century show members of the court playing the game. From China, like most good ideas it spread to Japan, where it became known as *da-kyu*, meaning "hit the ball". A classical oriental poem describes a game of polo played by noblemen which attracted so much attention that the palace guards deserted their posts and had to be severely censured by the Mikado.

When a favourite relative and brilliant polo player was killed during a match, the tenth-century Chinese Emperor T'ai Tsu had all the other players beheaded. Fortunately, stories of such ruthlessness are few and over the centuries history tells of powerful leaders and their followers playing the game with enthusiasm: Ming-huang, the "Radiant Emperor" of China; Harun-al-Rashid, the Islamic Caliph who maintained a *jukandar* or polo master; Qutub-ub-din-Aibak, the Indian king for whom there is a monument in Lahore where he died impaled on the ornate horn of his own saddle after a fall playing polo; the great Mongol conquerors Genghis Khan, whose men learned the game when they swept through Asia Minor, and Tamerlane, who is said to have ordered his cavalry to play with the heads of their enemies; Babur, the fifteenth-century Moghul who established the popularity of polo in India; Akbar the Great, whose vast polo stables can still be seen near Agra in northern India.

Historical evidence for the popularity of polo is found in lavishly illustrated writings, the work of painters, poets and historians who, with contemporary artisans, left manuscripts and works of art to tell the story. Shah Abbās left an even greater monument: the city of Isfahan created around his polo ground. The capital city of the Persian Safavid kingdom was moved there at the end of the sixteenth century and the Shah decided that it was to be the most beautiful in the Orient. The central square, the *maidan-i-shah*, became the royal polo ground with goal posts which can still be seen, eight yards apart, at each end – still the regulation width for a modern polo goal-mouth. The seven-storey Ali Qapu palace was built overlooking the halfway line and from its elaborate galleries the game could be enjoyed.

Below THE GAME WAS OFTEN DEPICTED IN CONTEMPORARY ILLUMINATED MANUSCRIPTS SUCH AS THIS SIXTEENTH CENTURY PERSIAN EXAMPLE.

With the collapse of the Eastern empires the game went into a decline and only survived in odd pockets. On the Indian subcontinent – where it was rediscovered by Westerners in the mid-nineteenth century – polo is not recorded at all during the seventeenth and eighteenth centuries. This, despite the fact that the Moghul emperors enjoyed it as a national sport until at least the end of the sixteenth century. The Tibetans probably picked the game up from the Chinese and it was from there that the Manipuris adopted polo. It was widely played throughout the district with each village having its own team. Europeans came across the sport when they came to the area to plant tea in the early 1850s and it was not long before they too were enjoying its delights.

Soon after the 1857 Mutiny, Joseph Sherer, a subaltern in the Indian Army, was posted to the Cachar District of Assam as Commandant of the Kookee Levy and Assistant Superintendent of the District. With the District Superintendent, Captain Robert Stewart, Sherer experienced his first taste of the Manipuri mounted game. Immediately taken with the sport he proposed that they form a club. Thus it was that in 1859 Sherer, Stewart and seven tea planters set up the first club of the modern game – the Silchar Polo Club. Other founding members of the club in this outpost of Empire were James Abernethy, Arthur Brownlow, James Davidson, Ernest Echardt, Julius Sandeman, A Stuart and W. Walker. They joined the local Manipuris for their 7-a-side regular games played on small ponies and seem to have become reasonably proficient. A couple of years elapsed before other Europeans noticed what was happening in this somewhat remote district, and it was not until 1861 that a Captain Eustace Hill took the game to Dacca and C. B. Stewart and some Calcutta merchants introduced it to their city.

Joe Sherer visited Calcutta in 1863 and once again became the catalyst for the setting up of a club – the Calcutta Polo Club – which proudly holds the title of the oldest club still in existence. A year later Sherer brought a visiting team of Manipuris, called the Band of Brothers, to Calcutta – a journey of two weeks. Playing on handy little ponies of about 11.2 hands, the Brothers easily beat the less well-mounted or experienced Calcutta club team. They returned home having sold many of their ponies for good prices and leaving an enthusiasm for polo which was to spread rapidly.

By 1865 the game had taken root in Bengal and by 1870 had spread throughout British India. Soon reports of the "new" game began to appear in British publications and it was in 1869 that an officer of the 10th Hussars, stationed at the time in Aldershot, England, was reading the *Field* magazine after lunch. There he read of the game and immediately initiated an afternoon's sport with his fellow officers. "Chicken" Hartopp, T.A. St. Quintin and others mounted their chargers and with walking sticks and a billiard ball attempted to play "hockey on horseback"; not, it must be said, with a great deal of success. The game appealed enough, however, for them to improvise a more useful stick, to produce specially turned balls and eventually to buy 17 small, handy ponies from Ireland expressly for the playing of polo.

Fellow officers from the 9th Lancers were introduced to the sport and in 1869 the first inter-regimental match on an English ground was played on Hounslow Heath. Even at

this early stage of the game, a newspaper reported that "Nearly all fashionable London" journeyed out to witness it. Playing eight to a side on 12½ hands high ponies, the game lasted for an hour and a half. The Household Cavalry soon took an interest in the game and tournaments quickly became a regular feature of Army life.

Left VIJAY SINGH, CAPTAIN OF THE CALCUTTA POLO CLUB. *Below* A MANIPURI TEAM POSE SOMEWHAT SELF-CONSCIOUSLY FOR A WESTERN PHOTOGRAPHER. THEIR HANDY LITTLE PONIES WERE MUCH SOUGHT AFTER.

In 1872 the 10th Hussars were posted to India, as were the 9th Lancers in 1875. With them they took the more sophisticated version of the game which had developed within a few years in England. The game as found in Manipur continued to be played in its rough state right up to World War II in some parts of India, but from the very first the European influence affected the way in which polo was conducted. Rules from Silchar formulated in 1863 sensibly regulated the game but also found it necessary to include that "It is to be understood that no player shall be under the influence of bhang, ganja or spiritous liquors". In 1876 St. Quintin called a meeting in Delhi to draw up a set of rules under which regimental polo was to be played. These included having only four players on each side.

At about the same time polo was beginning to be played at Hurlingham in London and it was there that a set of rules was drawn up which were to become almost universally accepted, with the governing body of the British game eventually becoming the Hurlingham Polo Association. John Watson, an Anglo-Irishman who played polo with the Carlow team in Ireland and the 13th Hussars in India, helped develop further guidelines for the discipline of the game and was a leading light on the Hurlingham committee. More importantly, however, his personal brilliance and skill helped to transform polo from its early somewhat scrappy style into a fast and thrilling team game.

Following the lead of the Army, fashionable people began to want to play and new polo clubs sprang up: at Lillie Bridge, Ranelagh, Wimbledon and Roehampton in and around London; at the first country club in Monmouthshire; and at many other places throughout the British Isles. It has been estimated that by the turn of the century in Greater London there were more than 10,000 ponies stabled – an indication of the extraordinary growth in popularity of the sport.

British Royal Navy officers also took to polo at this time when the horse was still important in everybody's lives. In 1874 the Malta Club was founded, listing among its players Lieutenant Prince Louis of Battenberg, later to become Admiral of the Fleet the Marquess of Milford Haven. Within ten years the club was able to list almost 100 playing members.

Above MEMBERS OF THE TOURING BELGIAN POLO TEAM RELAXING SOMEWHERE IN INDIA IN 1907. *Right above* AS THE SPORT BECAME ESTABLISHED BY THE BRITISH IN INDIA, MANY LOCAL NATIVE RULERS AND THEIR COURTS PROUDLY TOOK UP POLO. *Right below* PART OF THE GLORY OF INDIAN POLO IN THE 1920S: THE "TIGER" TEAM, HERE LED BY COUNT JOHN DE MADRE, PLAYED MANY INTERNATIONAL MATCHES.

Captain St. Quintin of the 10th Hussars and his brother took polo to Australia in 1876 and the first ground was laid out in Sydney a few years later after local civilians had taken up the game. Soon it travelled to New Zealand and Tasmania. South Africa had learned of the game in 1875 when teams from the Gordon Highlanders, the Duke of Cornwall's Light Infantry and the Cape Mounted Rifles played their first game there. In South America the game arrived with the British and was first played – also in 1875 – on David Shennans' *estancia* at El Negrete. The local cattle ranchers immediately saw the possibilities of the game and took to it with enthusiasm, setting up clubs in and around Buenos Aires, including the Hurlingham Club.

With such phenomenal growth it was clearly not going to be long before polo reached North America. In 1875 the newspaper publisher James Gordon Bennett, a keen sportsman, saw his first game of polo at the Hurlingham Club in England. A man of decision – he it was who sent Stanley to find Livingstone – Bennett returned to his native America with a set of sticks and balls and a strong dsire to organise the setting up of a number of teams. He sent the New York equestrian Harry Blosson to Texas to purchase suitable ponies and with 14 associates began organising teams. In the winter of 1876, the first formal demonstration game was played indoors at Dickel's Riding Academy in New York. When the weather and proficiency improved, outdoor games took place at the Jerome Park racetrack in Westchester County between teams captained by Bennett and Lord Mandeville, an Englishman living in America.

These polo grounds later became the home of the New York Giants baseball team and the club moved to Newport, Rhode Island, in 1879. By this time, Bennett had sold his ponies and moved out of the game but already it had taken a firm hold among the rich of the East coast and other clubs were being formed. The famous Meadow Brook Club was founded on Long Island and H. L. Herbert, the first chairman of the United States Polo

Association, started the Brighton Club (using croquet mallets extended on hayrake handles as he was unable at first to find proper sticks).

The Buffalo Polo Club of upstate New York also came into being, and in 1877 members took part in the first match between opposing clubs when they travelled to Westchester to be soundly beaten by the home side. This eight-a-side game was played with primitive equipment and no protective gear. The combatants must have been slow by modern standards but the match did excite those lucky enough to witness the event.

The first American public match was staged the following year on a newly-laid-out ground at Prospect Park, Brooklyn. Now with five players on each side, the Westchester club met a Queen's County Club team which fielded one of the greatest names of world polo – Thomas Hitchcock Senior – who had learned to play the game while studying at England's Oxford University. A crowd of 10,000 turned up to enjoy the spectacle, which was reported in one of the following day's newspapers as a "wild galloping, charging, thrusting game".

At this time in the USA, rules for the safety and comfort of ponies and players were far from settled and it would be some time before enthusiasts got together to formalise the game. Nevertheless, polo continued to spread and members of the general public were encouraged to enjoy it as a spectator sport. They, like their counterparts in other countries, were excited to witness many superb players – displaying new-found polo skills on better and better trained ponies – pursuing the ancient sport which, in its modern form, was taking the world by storm.

Left POLO AT JEROME PARK IN 1876, NOT LONG AFTER THE GAME HAD BEEN INTRODUCED TO AMERICA. *Above* THE GRANDSON OF THE CARPENTER WHO MADE HIS FIRST POLO BALL ONE HUNDRED YEARS BEFORE WAS STILL MANUFACTURING THEM AT HALSTEAD IN ESSEX WELL INTO THE TWENTIETH CENTURY.

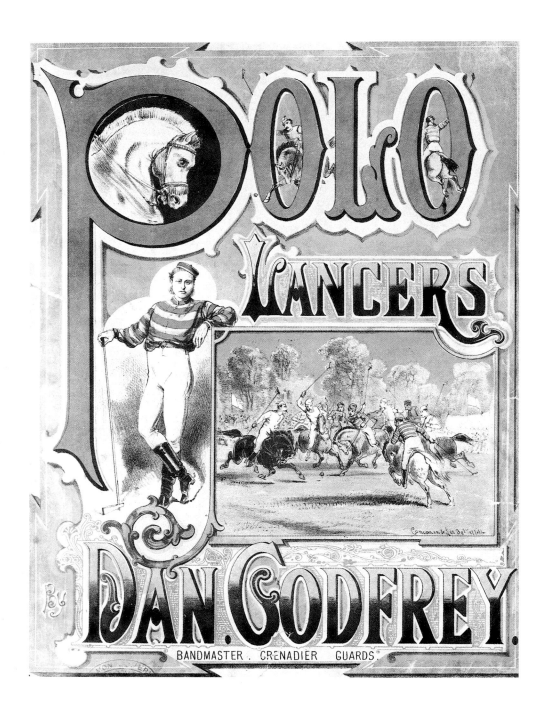

POLO WAS TO PROVE AN INSPIRATION FOR MANY THINGS,
INCLUDING THIS LIVELY PIECE OF BAND MUSIC.

2

THE GAME COMES OF AGE

As the old century entered its final decade, the feeling that polo might be only a passing fashion was constantly being disproved. In 1890 the future United States president Theodore Roosevelt was writing to a friend: "I tell you a corpulent middle-aged literary man finds a stiff polo match rather good exercise." Many of his contemporaries were taking up the game and new clubs were being founded throughout the US. This burgeoning popularity led to a need to standardise the rules and, under the chairmanship of H. L. Herbert, in 1890 the USPA (United States Polo Association) came into being.

A system of handicapping had been introduced in 1888 in order to equalise play and Herbert was assigned the role of official handicapper. Rated at this time between zero and 10 for their skill rather than their scoring ability, players and their clubs were often in dispute. The new association quickly took control of the situation. Along with Herbert on the governing board were such highly respected men as John Cowdin, Oliver Bird, Douglas Robinson and E. C. Potter.

As the ruling body for American polo began to take charge, meetings were held, usually twice a year, and seem to have been convivial affairs – the smart New York Café Savarin proving a favourite with board members. Other meetings took place at the Equitable Building and the Lawyers Club.

Changes in the rules were initiated and tournaments organised. Debate was hot as various controversies reared up. The number and duration of chukkas in a game was one of the first things that needed to be normalised. Writing about those times, the great Foxhall Keene recalled, "We used to play 20 minute periods which were killing. They were soon cut down to 15 and then to 10 . . . finally they came up with the $7\frac{1}{2}$ minute period . . . This has indubitably made polo much more popular and is probably a good thing for the game."

Experience was the chief factor in rule-change decisions and, as on the whole this was the same wherever polo was played, the US Polo Association based its first formal rules on those set out by the Hurlingham Club in 1875. Thus America played its part in the evolution of the game that in all parts of the world was coming of age. Organising bodies were regulating polo – and in consequence it was becoming increasingly more accessible.

In the USA, the "Glorious Sport of Polo", as *Mumsey's Magazine* had it, was continuing to expand. New clubs were being formed, attracting ever-increasing numbers of spectators – even if press coverage was sometimes less than enthusiastic. Most of the new clubs sprang up in the East, but soon spread throughout the continent. The Myopia Polo Club came out of the Boston club formed in 1884; in 1890 Theodore Roosevelt helped found the Oyster Bay

MAJOR GEORGE S. PATTON (CENTRE) WITH HIS TEAM. FOR HIM THE
ELEMENT OF PERSONAL RISK WAS "NOT A DRAWBACK, BUT A DECIDED ADVANTAGE."

Polo Club. James Gordon Bennett was still heavily involved and organising teams at Rockaway Hunt Club, Morris County, Essex County and the Narragansett Club in Massachusetts.

Polo began to be played in newly formed clubs on Staten Island and Saratoga in New York, Rhode Island, Brookline and Dedham in Massachusetts, Aiken and Camden in South Carolina, Devon in Pennsylvania and Somerset County in New Jersey. Also at that time, the game was introduced into California, St. Louis, Chicago, Colorado Springs and Denver. And the opening years of the new century in the US witnessed a polo-playing President in the White House and over 20 clubs with an enthusiastic membership of 300 players – all governed by the young US Polo Association.

The American armed forces were relatively late in starting their interest – even though much of the rest of the polo world was dominated by the military. However,

Squadron A of New York City took the game on and by 1904 some 50 men had started to play. They had more players than any other US club, their own field and a string of 74 ponies at Van Cortlandt Park. Mounts could be rented cheaply at $1 and the part-time soldiers were encouraged to improve their riding skills and at the same time enjoy pursuing the sport.

Within a few years the War Department had sanctioned the sport as a "developer of men" and the game was incorporated into the curriculum of the United States Military Academy, West Point. A young officer instructor, George Patton – later to become one of America's most controversial World War II generals – spoke for many when he wrote (somewhat inelegantly) at that time: "The War Department, in encouraging polo, is doing a very economical thing; the civilian player by helping and supporting is not only doing a very sporting thing, but is also of vast assistance rendering more efficient a body of men on whom, should war recur, the honour of his country will depend."

Elsewhere in the world polo was also gaining ground. The widely travelled British took polo sticks and balls to all the outposts of their Empire – and beyond. This was still the age of the horse and many an odd mount was pressed into the service of the sport. India, the cradle of the modern game, formed the Indian Polo Association in 1892, issuing the Rules of Polo to govern play all over the vast subcontinent. The same year also saw the joining together of various Argentinian committees to set up the Polo Association of the River Plate, which ran the game in Argentina until 1923. When the Polo Association of the River Plate was founded there were already more Argentinian clubs than there were British. Both Englishmen and Americans helped promote the game in Brazil, Chile, Colombia and Uruguay, although none of the other South American countries possessed players as skilled as the Argentinians.

As the British Royal Navy patrolled the world's waters, so the game proliferated. From the splendid Malta Club, with its huge list of players drawn from the ranks of the Royal Navy, the game was taken far and wide. Teams from the Mediterranean Fleet played in Gibraltar, Cyprus, Egypt, Morocco, Tunisia, Algeria, Greece, Spain, France and Italy. At that time an American commentator, speaking of a British team, wrote, "The military sabre drill of the Englishman comes into good play in polo. They used the mallet with the same ferociously wicked sweep with which they would have slashed down the Egyptian rebels during the Sudan campaign."

During the Sudan campaign of the 1890s polo was played by officers from the Nile gunboats. One of those players – a young sub-lieutenant – went on to become Admiral of the Fleet Earl Beatty. In the West Indies, Commander HRH Prince George of Wales (afterwards King George V of England) was also frequently to be seen riding onto the polo field. On the China station, Naval teams played against men from the German Far East Squadron, which included Prince Henry of Prussia and the future World War I naval commander Maximilian Graf von Spee. Nigeria, South Africa, the Gold Coast and the islands of Mauritius, St. Helena and Cape Verde all provided locations for the game, many clubs being formed which have lasted to the present day, including those in Ghana (1902), Kenya (1903), and Nigeria (1904).

In 1888 five Royal Navy ships put into Auckland for the opening of New Zealand's north island Calliope Dock. Having learned the game in Malta, a few of the officers had brought sticks and balls with them and thus it was that the Auckland Polo Club was formed in the summer of that year. Teddy O'Rorke, son of the Speaker in the House of Representatives, took up the sport with some of his local friends and soon transferred it to Christchurch in the South Island. A national trophy – given by and named after British army officer R. F. Savile, who was ADC to the Governor – was first played for in 1890 between the Auckland and Christchurch clubs. Enthusiasm for polo, roused by the Savile Cup and other competitions, grew and the New Zealand Polo Association was founded in 1898.

In Australia, from its beginnings in 1875, polo had flourished – thanks to a plentiful supply of local ponies and encouragement from English visitors. One such was Captain Douglas Haig (afterwards Field-Marshal Earl Haig), who drew up the "polo code and hints for players" in New South Wales. As in so many of the places where it was booming, in Australia polo tended to be taken up by those who had an abundance of land and horses – rather than by the monied city dwellers.

On the European continent polo was attracting more and more enthusiasts in Germany, Spain, France, Austria, Italy, Poland, Hungary and even as far afield as Russia. There were very few places that itinerant polo players (who tended to be of the class that travelled in style) could not find convivial company prepared to lend them ponies and provide exciting games. Along with this phenomenally quick spread of the sport came a general understanding and standardisation of the rules. By the end of the nineteenth century international matches were being played and the fame of the more outstanding players was beginning to spread.

JAMES GORDON BENNETT, THE NEWSPAPER MAN WHO IS CREDITED WITH
BRINGING POLO TO AMERICA, AS CARICATURED IN VANITY FAIR MAGAZINE.

FOXHALL KEENE, CAPTAIN OF THE AMERICAN TEAM AND BRILLIANT
INTERNATIONAL PLAYER, WHO WROTE EXTENSIVELY ABOUT THE GAME.

The Westchester Cup was the first of the great transcontinental internationals. Surprise had been expressed in 1886 when the American player Griswold Lorillard told his dinner hosts at the Hurlingham Club in London that polo was played in the United States. It did not take long before a challenge to play a series of matches was issued and the Westchester Club agreed to meet all the English team expenses. They also offered a cup "to be emblematic of a polo championship of the two countries".

Sending their ponies on before them, the Hurlingham team sailed for New York in August of that year. The captain, John Watson, was joined by three army officers, the Hon. Richard Lawley and Thomas Hone of the 7th Hussars and Malcolm Little of the 9th Lancers. In New York they were greeted by the American team of Raymond Belmont, W. K. Thorn and two men who were later to become top-rated 10-goal players: Thomas Hitchcock and Foxhall P. Keene.

The match consisted of a punishing three chukkas – each lasting 30 minutes – and contemporary newspaper and magazine reports told of the English playing like clockwork and the Americans being too individualistic. The New York Herald, Gordon Bennett's paper, reported: "... it was natural cleverness against trained skill, and in polo you may bet to the bottom of your pocket on the latter."

"I attribute our success," said Captain Watson of the Hurlingham team, in an interview after the game (in which the score was 10-4 to the British), "first to the superiority of our ponies, and secondly to our skill as a team in collective playing." The British had gained their first polo victory over the Americans, and it was agreed that subsequent matches for the Westchester Cup would be played in the country of the winning team under that country's rules.

Foxhall Keene was later to state that, despite this American defeat, the games themselves had laid the cornerstone of modern polo. Much effort was put into improving the American team's pony power and in 1900 Keene took a squad consisting of himself, F. J. Mackay and Lawrence and Walter McCreery to play in England at the Hurlingham Club. But they were no match for John Watson and his winning team of Frederick Freake, Captain the Hon. J. E. Beresford and Walter Buckmaster – another player who was to achieve the coveted 10-goal handicap rating – losing 8-2 in the formal Anglo-American match.

It was not until 1902 that the Americans felt that they could challenge for the second Westchester Cup series, and five men crossed the Atlantic with their ponies: Keene, John Cowdin, Rodolphe Agassiz and the brothers Monty and Larry Waterbury – all eventual 10-goal handicapped players. Against them the Hurlingham committee put Freake, Buckmaster, P. and C. Nickalls and C. D. Miller (who did not play because of injury). The Americans won the first game but despite high hopes lost the next two, thus leaving the cup in British hands. John Cowdin considered that again it was the "invariable and consummate position play" of the English that helped them to dominate the games.

A few years after their dispirited return home, the US national team came under the firm leadership of Harry Payne Whitney of Meadow Brook. He was determined to achieve victory. By improving training techniques, providing better than ever ponies, and changing to the use

POLO.
At 4.0.
SECOND
INTERNATIONAL MATCH.

AMERICA CHALLENGE CUP.

U.S. AMERICA *v.* **ENGLAND.**

Mr. L. Waterbury.	(1)	Mr. H. Rich.
Mr. M. Waterbury.	(2)	Mr. F. M. Freake.
Mr. H. P. Whitney.	(3)	Mr. P. W. Nickalls.
Mr. D. Milburn.	(*back*)	Capt. Hardress Lloyd.
(*Blue and White.*)		(*Dark Blue and Red Rose.*)

ꓛ০০০০০০০০০০০০

UMPIRES :

America	...	Captain E. D. Miller, D.S.O.
England	...	Major K. Maclaren, D.S.O.

Referee : Mr. W. S. Buckmaster.

of the British rule which allowed stick hooking, the American national squad was ready to challenge again in 1909.

Payne Whitney took with him to England the Waterbury brothers and Devereux Milburn. The "Big Four" had arrived on the scene – all destined to become 10-goal handicapped players. For this trip they were superbly mounted on a string of 28 ponies – many of which had been bought from the English. Their captain, said Foxhall Keene, "chased the Waterburys and Milburn around London like schoolboys and made sure they got in at a reasonable hour each evening".

All of Payne Whitney's hard work was vindicated when a British team, consisting of future 10-goalers Freake, Captain J. Hardress Lloyd and Lord Wodehouse – along with Captain Herbert Wilson, P. W. Nickalls and Harry Rich – were outclassed by the Big Four. As *The Times* reported somewhat laconically: "It may be said that the better team has won." They had won decisively the first two of the traditional Westchester "best of three" games which now consisted of six 10-minute chukkas. Payne Whitney had succeeded in training a team which, said T. F. Dale, "showed the possibilities of combination and discipline in a free galloping game".

Far left THE 1911 UNITED STATES AND BRITISH CAPTAINS FOR THE WESTCHESTER CUP SERIES, HARRY PAYNE WHITNEY AND CAPTAIN J. HARDRESS LLOYD. *Left* THE 1909 LINE-UP FROM THE ORIGINAL PROGRAMME. *Below* THE AMERICAN BIG FOUR WHO NEVER LOST TO ENGLAND: MILBURN, WHITNEY AND THE WATERBURY BROTHERS.

With the Westchester Cup now in America it was the British team's turn to cross the Atlantic in 1911 to take part in the next challenge. The United States had no offside rule and in anticipation of this the English suspended that particular regulation which was causing a slowing down of their game. Hardress Lloyd was captain of the team and took with him Wilson, Captain Noel Edwards and Captain Leslie Cheape, with Captain "Rattle" Barrett in reserve. The Americans again fielded the Big Four.

England's ponies were found to be wanting, despite the fact that 14 of the 35 taken had been bought by the specially formed American Cup Recovery Fund Committee – evidence of the esteem in which the competition was held by that time. Yet even with the Big Four playing on superior mounts victory did not come easily and America retained the cup by the skin of their teeth after two hard-fought games that ended with only ½ and one goal differences after eight 7½-minute chukkas.

Two years later, in 1913, a determined British returned with 42 ponies provided by the Duke of Westminster. With Buckmaster unavailable because of injury, Captain R. G. Ritson led the squad, which included Captains A. N. Edwards, Vivian Lockett and Leslie Cheape, with Freake in reserve. It was a strong team with Ritson, Lockett and Cheape all handicapped at 10 goals. The American team had also experienced a number of problems but in the end the Big Four eventually represented their country with Louis Stoddard, who was raised to a 10-goal handicap in 1922, replacing Monty Waterbury in the second match.

A series of excitingly close-fought games resulted in yet another victory for the Americans and G. D. Armour, the artist and polo player who covered the series for *Country Life* magazine, wrote admiringly of them: "I think the American influence speeded up polo as it did racing, and I am sure that the pace at which these international games go necessitates those taking part being in the youthful prime of life and absolutely fit to stand the strain entailed."

The British challenged again in the following year, taking out Cheape, Lockett, Barrett and Captain H. A. Tomkinson. The team looked powerful. Barrett was by now a 10-goal player and Lord Wimborne provided some excellent ponies. After a gap of five years the cup was once more returned to England when they beat an American line-up of the Waterbury brothers, Milburn and René La Montagne, Whitney having finally retired from international competition. The superior play of the British was all the more remarkable considering that the games were postponed for four days because Cheape had received a broken nose in practice before the main tournament.

The Westchester Cup games, played on the Meadow Brook ground, attracted large and fashionable crowds. In 1913 Armour noted that those in authority had allowed him to see the game from the boards along the side of the field which, while not perhaps providing the best view, did at least offer sight of the game "without obstruction from such things – if I may say so – as the expensive hats which ladies then used to wear".

Above POLO HAS ALWAYS BEEN A SPORT WHERE SPEED HAS BEEN OF
PARAMOUNT IMPORTANCE. NOEL EDWARDS MOUNTS A FRESH PONY
DURING A GAME WITH NOT A MOMENT TO SPARE.
Left THOMAS HITCHCOCK JR REMAINED A GOD OF AMERICAN POLO
FOR TWENTY YEARS. LIKE HIS FATHER HE WAS A 10-GOAL PLAYER.

Clearly international games were able to provide a new form of interest and excitement. Highly-rated foreign players were welcome wherever they travelled, and from the beginning polo assumed an international flavour. Britain's links with India – where polo could be played all the year round – meant that the game benefited greatly from the continual flow of servicemen to and from the subcontinent. Teams from the Argentine had been visiting since Hugh Scott-Robinson brought a team to England in 1896, entirely mounted on native-bred ponies, which won most of the games it played. In 1911 Joe and Johnny Traill, with J. A. Lynch-Staunton and H. Schwind, enjoyed similar success during a visit – giving notice that the Argentinians were a force to be reckoned with.

Other non-representative teams were also travelling long distances to play their chosen sport. The Coronado Country Club in California really took off when four British peers, Lord Tweedmouth, Lord Innes-Ker, Lord Reginald Herbert and Lord Lucien Gower, visited the state. Mounted on borrowed local ponies they so enjoyed their games there that they spread the word about the excellence of California as a winter venue for polo.

Polo was included in the Paris Olympic Games of 1900 and in 1908 in London. Able to enter more than one team, in 1900 Great Britain won both gold and silver medals with France taking the bronze. In 1908 the home teams took all three places and the medals. One of the silver medallists on that occasion was Lord Wodehouse who also played for his country in the next Olympic polo competition when Great Britain won the gold medal, beating Spain which took the silver and the United States which came third for the bronze in the 1920 Antwerp Games.

Polo made another Olympic appearance in 1924, again in Paris. By this time the Argentinians were dominating the game and they beat America into second place, with Great Britain trailing into third. The Berlin Games of 1936 saw another Argentinian victory, with Great Britain taking the silver medal and Mexico the bronze.

Great Britain's win in the 1914 Westchester Cup series was to be their last for some time. Soon Europe was at war and men and horses were pressed into active service. Foreign postings took on a grim aspect that was not conducive to the playing of polo. At this time, however – with Europeans and eventually the Americans embroiled in a massive armed conflict – the sport surged forward dramatically in the Argentine. Even in the US the popularity of the game continued and when the USPA introduced a pony registry in 1915, a total of 150 players registered nearly 700 animals with the Association. Each

pony was awarded a certificate stating that it met the then standard height requirement of 14.2 hands. By 1920 this regulation was to be abandoned and returning British players were presented with a *fait accompli* – accepted if only because all types of horses were in short supply after the slaughter of the Great War.

Another important development in the States at this time was the organisation of a number of clubs, led by the Piping Rock Club of New York, to encourage young players to improve their game. For example, members of the Metropolitan Polo Association between them bought a number of ponies and agreed to maintain them for use by younger and less affluent players. The scheme was an outstanding success and the general level of play improved as a result. Other associations soon followed suit and many newcomers from the rising business class were attracted to the sport and joined clubs.

The importance of encouraging the involvement of young players was recognised by the introduction of the game, through the officer training corps, into America's top universities. In 1918 Cornell began to play, followed a year later by Princeton and Yale. Soon a strong intercollegiate system developed and indoor polo also expanded in popularity at this time since many of the young players wanted to enjoy their newly-chosen sport all the year round.

The East coast clubs' dominance of the game had been increasingly challenged throughout the early years of the century and by 1917 polo was firmly established in the West and in the South. Even though Californian ponies were generally becoming accepted as the best, it was this East-West rivalry that needed to be tested, those in the East simply not believing that the "cowboys" from out West could possess any real polo talent. They were proven wrong when a team from Midwick, a fine club in Coronado, California, met with one from Cooperstown, New York, and soundly beat them – giving warning that good things were coming from the West.

Above A MEXICAN GOAL IS SCORED IN THE MATCH AGAINST ARGENTINA DURING THE 1936 BERLIN OLYMPIC GAMES. *Below* THE BIG FOUR OF THE 1920S WHO NEVER LOST AN INTERNATIONAL MATCH: MILBURN, STEVENSON, HITCHCOCK AND WEBB.

J. WATSON WEBB, THE WORLD'S ONLY LEFT-HANDED 10-GOALER. NOW ALL
PLAYERS MUST HOLD THE STICK IN THEIR RIGHT HAND.

Throughout the countries of Europe, hundreds of potentially talented players had perished on the Great War battlefields but those who did return took every opportunity to live their lives – and their polo – to the full. The Prince of Wales and his brother the Duke of York both enjoyed the game. The very popular and dashing Prince Edward (later King Edward VIII and then Duke of Windsor), known to his family and friends as David, took every opportunity to play wherever he found himself and his enthusiastic participation did much to popularise the game. Perhaps Prince Edward's greatest contribution, though, was to introduce his cousin – the young Louis Mountbatten – to the game of polo.

On Thursday 1 December 1921, writing in a diary kept whilst accompanying Prince Edward on a tour to India, Mountbatten made the following entry: "This day is a red letter one for me, as besides getting my first pig [he had spent the morning pigsticking] I played my first game of polo. I played in two chukkas, the 8th and the 11th . . . I was playing on the Maharaja's side against David [the Prince of Wales], and, of course, it was due to the latter

that I was playing at all. In the last chukka, to my own intense surprise, I actually hit the ball three or four times. Anyway I loved it and hope to get lots more."

Mountbatten did indeed ensure that he got "lots more" and was instrumental in promoting the game throughout the rest of his long and eventful life, introducing both his nephew Prince Philip and his great-nephew Prince Charles to the game. He also wrote one of the most important and influential text books on the game, *An Introduction to Polo*, which first appeared in 1931 and has been in print ever since.

In New Zealand after the war polo was recovering, with help from men such as Robert Levin who organised the country's first national ground at Feilding on North Island. By 1929 the number of active clubs had grown from its pre-war level of nine to 16. In another part of the British Empire the Indian Rajput aristocracy were also doing much to encourage the growth of the game.

In England itself, postwar recovery was slow, due to a combination of a lack of good players – such great names as Leslie Cheape, Noel Edwards, Herbert Wilson and the

Grenfell twins had fallen in the conflict – and the fact that the British were now generally poorer than their foreign counterparts and the stock of good mounts was low. But polo was still popular as a sport and attracted great crowds wherever it was played. If the standard was not as high as it had been, enthusiasm was as great.

The "Roaring twenties" was a period of considerable change. On both sides of the Atlantic men and women were entering into the world of polo with gusto. Top players were becoming stars – and it did not seem to matter where they came from. There was a greater informality; social barriers were breaking down. Polo was undergoing a renaissance – entering its "Golden Years" – and the two decades between the two world wars saw the emergence of some of the greatest players, thrilling huge crowds on fine-bred ponies that were beginning to command high prices – indicating their true worth to the game.

First among the new breed of players in Britain was the brilliant Rao Rajah Hanut Singh from Jodhpur in India. Son of a polo-playing father, it was said that he used to practise by hitting a ball to and from school. After serving as the youngest officer of the Jodhpur Lancers during the Great War, he returned to India to play off a handicap of 5 in the 1918 Delhi tournament. Within a month he had been raised to 8 and by 1919 Hanut was rated at 9 goals.

The visiting US Westchester Cup team of 1921 demonstrated only too well just how far behind the British game had fallen. Star of that side was the son of a polo-playing father and mother, Tommy Hitchcock Jr. Mrs Hitchcock was captain of her own team and doing much to encourage the new generation of young players in the States. The 10-goal handicapped Devereux Milburn as captain completed his team with two others who, besides Hitchcock, were the following year to be raised to a 10-goal rating: J. Watson Webb and Louis Stoddard.

Ranged against them on ponies again provided by Lord Wimborne were three men from the victorious 1914 team – Lockett, Tomkinson and Barrett – and Lord Wodehouse, a 10-goaler. They looked good on paper but when it came to the match were crushingly defeated in two straight games. Contributing to their discomfiture was the excellence of the American ponies, many of which had been bought at great expense from the Argentines.

When, three years later, Meadow Brook proved the site for another easy victory for the American team, the British Hurlingham committee delegated the task of choosing a team for the 1927 series to the Army in India Association, recognising that in that country British polo was at its strongest. Unaccountably leaving out the great Hanut, the

Association chose Majors E. G. Atkinson and Austin Williams, Captains J. P. Dening, C. T. I. Roark, Claude Pert and R. George.

This new British team was better mounted than its predecessors, thanks mainly to the Maharajahs of Jodhpur and Ratlam. Unfortunately they came up against what was probably the finest polo team ever assembled – the Big Four of the twenties – Devereux Milburn, Malcolm Stevenson, Tommy Hitchcock and J. Watson Webb. Despite losing the two games, the British acquitted themselves well, earning extra praise for their gentlemanly behaviour. In the second game Stevenson was badly injured when a ball hit him on the left knee-cap. Returning to the field his opposite number, Captain George, asked which leg had been hurt and thereafter studiously avoided riding him off on that side, despite the advantage this gave to the Americans.

The British run of bad luck continued in 1930 when, despite fielding a formidable team of Gerald Balding, Louis Lacey, C. T. I. Roark and Humphrey P. Guinness, the Americans were again simply a stronger side. Hitchcock was this time joined by Earl Hopping, Winston Guest (a 10-goal indoor player) and Eric Pedley. Although the son of a British army officer and grandson of two generals, Pedley was hailed by the press as a "Texas Cowboy" brought from obscurity into the international arena. This was certainly stretching the truth for someone brought up on a ranch just outside Los Angeles and already a well-known polo player, but it fitted well into the growing awareness that polo was no longer dominated by the monied aristocrats of the East.

Polo in the US continued to grow and prosper. Texas was undoubtedly becoming a polo state with the classic combination seen in Latin America: an abundance of good horses plus a people used to riding from early childhood. The rancher and horse dealer George Miller led the Austin and Camp polo team, renowned for its seemingly inexhaustible supply of pony power. Most teams had more than 40 mounts to call upon and they all played a lot of polo. At the end of the 1926 season one Texan player concluded that he had travelled 77 miles for each game, covering thousands of miles during the season.

Players from the northeast had the advantage of wintering in California and Florida, where the northern sportsman Carl Fisher was helping to develop Miami as the winter capital of polo. Here – as elsewhere throughout the US – crowds of spectators turned out to enjoy the games and it was not unusual to see as many as 5,000 at the big matches.

By the end of the 1930s – and with up to 40,000 in the stands – polo was undeniably popular in the US. The writer Damon Runyon attended many international matches at this time and his trained eye saw much – both off as well as on the field of play: "The brisk cavalry charge of the American four at Meadow Brook swept the British challengers from the turfed field . . . There was rodeo riding on both sides and, in the tangles of men and horses, luck often helped the Stars and Stripes . . . Pedley is the first man from the West to play in an international four, and he won enough glory today to give each state beyond the Mississippi a fair share."

Off the field he noted acres of automobiles and "the mob of hustlers and souvenir vendors that follow every big Eastern sporting event . . . As early as 1 p.m. there were little picnic parties spread out on the grass behind the stands, munching hard-boiled eggs, ham sandwiches and what-not. Chiefly what-not. At first glance it seemed as if the most aristocratic event in American sport might be going democratic, but closer scrutiny of what they were eating disclosed them as real blue bloods. They had no salami in their picnic baskets."

The "Social Register" and "Who's Who" were both well represented at Meadow Brook, along with many "bigwigs" from England. Reserved seats cost $13.75 but general admission could be obtained for as little as $2 – so the game was within the reach of most. Polo seemed to have been unaffected by the Wall Street Crash of 1929 – perhaps because the real enthusiasts had spent more time in the saddle than speculating on the Bull Market.

Runyon may have been right that polo was mainly for "blue bloods", but its growing popularity was having an effect on the media. Press coverage of the game had never been greater. The 1926 American Open was featured by the then new National Broadcasting Corporation in its first year of operation. The first *Polo* magazine had been started in 1927 and within a few years games were being recorded on film for showing alongside the new and popular talking movies.

To help with identification, numbered jerseys began to be adopted during the 1920s. As the game became faster and more dangerous, protective headgear was increasingly being used and kneeguards were soon standard issue as players learned to ride off more fiercely to gain advantage. Polo sticks were being designed to suit individual players' specifications and an interchange of ideas meant that gradually the head was redesigned from the early square block to a cigar shape. The long handles were better balanced and had a superior grip.

Polo ponies of an extraordinarily high standard were being bred and this was demonstrated beyond doubt when the Argentines entered the international arena, playing the first of the Cup of the Americas series in 1928. It had been proposed that they join in the Westchester Cup tournaments but as this had always been intended to be an Anglo-American competition the Copa de las Americas was instituted instead.

Although the Cup of the Americas was won by the United States in its inaugural year and again in 1932, it proved tough going and the excellence of the Argentinian horses was noted. Tommy Hitchcock led the 1928 team which included Earl Hopping, Malcolm Stevenson, Winston Guest and one of the most astute diplomats of his generation, W. Averell Harriman. They met with Arturo Kenny, Juan Nelson, J. B. Miles and Louis Lacey. In 1932 the Copa de las Americas was played for in Buenos Aires and the home team consisted of Kenny and Nelson, joined by Martin and José Reynal and Manual Andrada. The USPA sent another strong team to defend their previous victory: Michael Phipps, Elmer Boeseke, William Post and Winston Guest. They won two of the three matches but again it was a close-fought tournament.

The 1932 match proved to be the USA's final victory over the Argentines, who were well mounted and played with a skill that was to lead to their taking the polo world by storm. By the 1930s a number of families in South America were producing brilliant young players. These were being given every facility to play on the best of ponies and their world-beating quality was beginning to show.

A TOP WINNING TEAM: PAUL BUTLER, CECIL SMITH, HAROLD BARRY AND JACKIE MURPHY WITH ALAN HOWARD.

On the other side of the world an Australian family was coming to the attention of the polo fraternity. During the 1920s at the Goulburn club, four brothers had begun to play polo and, backed by their sheep-farming parents, they formed a team which played together until 1939. Jim, Bob, Geoff and Phil Ashton typified the essentially rural nature of the sport in Australasia. Using ponies which were also stock working animals, they became excellent players because they loved the sport – not because they were socially ambitious. Geoff Ashton attributed the team's strength to the fact that they lived, talked – and always played – together.

By 1930 the Ashtons had taken over as leading team in New South Wales from the Harden team of A. C. McLaurin and the three brothers Knox, Bill and Tom Ross. So in that year they decided to travel to England to play for a season with their own string of ponies. And thus they made an extraordinary two-month voyage on a small wooden-decked ship with 25 horses – and a great deal of faith.

Each day three of the Ashtons led the mounts from their specially constructed loose boxes wearing shoes made of non-slip mat to a little sand-based exercise yard. After facing many storms and 13,500 miles of sea they arrived in England to meet up with their mother and brother Bob who, a bad sailor, had come by ocean liner. Within a week the Goulburn team was playing a good standard of polo on ponies which seemed none the worse for the voyage.

Amazingly they reached the final of the Hurlingham Championship Cup and although they did not win, their father James Ashton received a special trophy from King Alfonso of Spain, who was presenting the prizes that year and was immensely impressed with the Australians' adventure. Other polo enthusiasts were similarly affected and the Ashtons were asked to play a series of games in America. Adopting the same spirit of adventure that had brought them to England, they sailed to New York, aware this time, however, that they would be able to sell their ponies in the States and recoup some of their expenses. Having won five of the seven matches that they played, the sale of their ponies raised a colossal $77,000 – and many admiring newspaper headlines.

The Ashton polo odyssey did much to put Australia on the map and having continued to play brilliantly on their return to New South Wales, they went back to England in 1937. With Bob Skene replacing Phil, they finally won the Hurlingham Championship Cup, for which they had only been runners-up seven years previously.

LOUIS LACEY; BORN IN CANADA OF BRITISH PARENTS HE LIVED MOST
OF HIS LIFE IN ARGENTINA. LACEY'S 10-GOAL TALENTS WERE USED BY
BOTH BRITAIN AND HIS SOUTH AMERICAN HOMELAND.

During the 1930s, polo in the East of America was dominated by a number of fabulously rich families – all of whom supported large strings of ponies. Among the 40 or so high-goal players Laddie Sanford was heir to a multimillion dollar carpet company, Seymour S. Knox inherited a fortune from the Woolworth estate, and R. E. Sawbridge derived his wealth from department stores in Philadelphia. They and others enjoyed family riches undreamed of by most.

Family involvement was great, with fathers and sons, brothers and cousins, all playing the game – often to a high level. The Hitchcocks, the Milburns, the Guests, the Phipps, the Hays, the Shermans, the Igleharts, all were active and influential in polo at this time. Power was definitely concentrated in the East and from the foundation of the USPA in 1890 until 1950, the five men who served as chairman were all part of the Eastern establishment: H. L. Herbert (1890–1921), W. A. Hazard (1921–2), Louis Stoddard (1922–36), R. E. Sawbridge Jr. (1936–40, 1946–50) and Elbridge Gerry (1940–46).

The Eastern hegemony was, however, under threat – from the Western ranchers and cowboys who were bringing up their working ponies to play their chosen sport – men with the same stamp of dedication as the Ashton brothers. Their challenge came to a climactic head in 1933 with an East-West series played at the Onwentsia Polo Club, near Chicago, and at the future capital of American polo, Oak Brook.

The West, led by Eric Pedley, was really coming to be noticed in the polo world, thanks to a number of brilliant young players who could genuinely lay claim to the cowboy tradition. Rube Williams was a teacher and player of some skill, but by 1933 he was surpassed by his 29-year-old pupil Cecil Smith. Both had been raised on a ranch in Texas and had ridden since childhood, working and eventually playing their horses.

With Williams playing off an 8-goal handicap and Smith nine, they formed the nucleus of the Western team, which also included the 7-goalers Aiden Roark and Elmer Boeseke. The Eastern team fielded a well-established side captained by top 10-goal player Tommy Hitchcock. They were joined by the 8-goaler Winston Guest and his brother Raymond who, with the young Michael Phipps, was playing off a 7-goal handicap.

Media coverage for this battling East-West match series was widespread and it caught the imagination of the sporting public. The East team was strongly favoured but, although very much a "dark horse", the reputation of their opponents was high and everyone knew it would be a close-run thing. The games themselves were rough and incident-packed. In the first, Smith was knocked unconscious for 23 minutes after his horse rolled on him but he returned to score an important goal in the eighth and final chukka. Sensationally, the West won 15-11.

The next day's second game provided some nail-biting polo, although it proved unlucky for Rube Williams when he broke a leg in a jarring ride-off. He was replaced by Neil McCarthy and an urgent message was sent to Eric Pedley to fly to Chicago in case he was needed for the third game. The East won the second game 12-8, so Pedley's input was to prove vital.

The crucial third game of the series was the scene of yet another accident. Tommy Hitchcock fell badly, was concussed, and although he continued to play, his game was badly affected. Even so, the great man was able to score three goals. However these were not enough and the West took a 12-6 victory and for once and all let the world know that they had arrived firmly on the polo scene. It was not long before Cecil Smith's handicap was raised to 10 goals which, uniquely, he was to keep for a total of 25 years. Elmer Boeseke also held a 10-goal rating and thus by 1934 two of the three American 10-goalers – the other was Easterner Hitchcock – were from the West.

The famous humourist and commentator Will Rogers, himself a polo player, wrote about this match series: "The East never thought the West could muster up four guys with white pants, much less some mallets . . . Well, the hillbillies beat the dudes and took the polo championship right out of the drawing room and into the bunkhouse. The East always thought you had to have a fancy pedigree to play polo. Poor old society, nothing exclusive left."

Throughout the 1930s, polo was becoming more accessible to the ordinary spectator – thanks to men such as Pete Bostwick. Believing that the general public would be interested in watching the game, he threw open his private Long Island field, charging an entrance fee of 50 cents. The people came in great numbers, much to the surprise of many within the polo establishment. For the US Open matches of 1935 the USPA announced a public entrance fee of $1, representing a reduction of $10 on the previous lowest price. The public flocked in, adding much to the general ambience and excitement of the games. And those who came enjoyed some of the best polo the world could offer. By the mid-1930s, the US had a 40-goal "Dream Team" consisting of Hitchcock, Smith, Mike Phipps and Stewart Iglehart.

Iglehart had played polo at Yale and was a superb athlete and a dedicated sportsman, regularly riding his horses before going to work and practising shots from the wooden horse on his return. He became a member of the 1936 Westchester Cup team that travelled to England to meet a Great Britain side of Hesketh Hughes, Gerald Balding, Eric Tyrell Martin and Humprey Guinness. The games were played in England because of the Hurlingham Polo Association's financial problems, resulting in their inability to send a team out to the States. Along with Iglehart came Eric Pedley, Mike Phipps and Winston Guest – and 53 ponies, half American bred and half Argentinian.

Two seven-chukka games were played in June, with a gap of ten days between them, necessitated by a combination of rain and the Royal Ascot race meeting. Crowds of eight and twelve thousand turned out to watch the US team beat their opponents in two games and the Royal Box was graced with the presence of, among others, the Duke and Duchess of Gloucester, Prince Arthur of Connaught and King Alfonso of Spain.

Meanwhile in America, the Argentinians, fresh from their Olympic victory, decisively beat a team consisting of Hitchcock, Gerald Balding, Pete Bostwick and John Hay Whitney in the Copa de las Americas. While this marked a turning point in American polo supremacy, the standard was extraordinarily high. For the 1937 US Open – which as many as 20,000 spectators a day attended – six teams battled for the title. Among the players were most of the great names of the decade: Cecil Smith, Tommy Hitchcock, Raymond Guest, Mike Phipps, Gerald Balding, Pete Bostwick, Stewart Iglehart, Seymour Knox, Robert Sawbridge, Pat Roark, C. V. Whitney, John Hay Whitney, Winston Guest, William Post II and Elbridge and Robert Gerry.

Many of these players were shortlisted to defend the Westchester Cup in 1939. Eventually the US committee chose Phipps, Hitchcock, Iglehart and Winston Guest. In what was to be the last Westchester series, they met an England team of Aiden Roark, Gerald Balding, Eric Tyrell Martin and Bob Skene (who qualified because his native Australia was a member of the Commonwealth). Few were surprised that the Americans retained the cup and contemporary commentators on the sport offered their varied opinion on what was wrong with British polo. One thing was clear: morale was at a low ebb and everyone was aware that war threatened and could prove the end of an era.

Even though in India the rajahs were maintaining teams with considerable strings of ponies and cavalry regiments could call on a pool of up to 500 troop horses for the officers' polo games (which had a favourable effect on polo

in England), yet it was known that this could not last. Army life had to change in the face of the Nazi threat. The thunder of hooves gave way to the roar of tanks and the whine of sinister aircraft. The outbreak of a second world war meant that polo would never be the same again. The "Golden Age" was over – but all was not lost.

Right above THE 40 GOAL 'DREAM TEAM': STEWART IGLEHART, TOMMY HITCHCOCK, CECIL SMITH AND MIKE PHIPPS. *Right below* ARGENTINIAN WINNERS OF THE 1936 OLYMPIC CHAMPIONSHIP AND THE CUP OF THE AMERICAS: MANUEL ANDRADA, ANDRES GASSOTTI, ROBERTO CAVANAGH AND LUIS DUGGAN. *Below* THE POLO-PLAYING BROTHERS FRANK AND THOMAS HITCHCOCK, PHOTOGRAPHED AFTER FRANK RETURNED TO THE GAME FOLLOWING AN ALMOST FATAL ACCIDENT.

Left THE ARRIVAL OF THE INTERNATIONAL POLO CHALLENGE CUP ABOARD THE SS AMERICAN BANKER IN 1936 ATTRACTED PUBLIC ATTENTION AND THE BRITISH-AMERICAN MATCHES THAT YEAR DREW LARGE CROWDS. **Below left** A MEMBER OF LA ESPADANA TEAM FROM THE ARGENTINE CHATS TO HIS GAUCHO GROOM AFTER HAVING LOST TO HURLINGHAM AT ROEHAMPTON IN 1951. **Below** POLO PASSIONS CONTINUE FOR MANY YEARS, AS DEMONSTRATED BY THIS PICTURE OF 81-YEAR-OLD MISS KATHERINE FOOT, ABOUT TO GO OUT FOR A PRACTICE CHUKKA AT HAM, ENGLAND, IN 1933. **Right** IN 1937 AMERICA PRODUCED A TEAM OF PLAYERS FROM THE YAKIMA TRIBE. WHETHER THEY ACTUALLY PLAYED IN THEIR MAGNIFICENT HEADDRESSES IS NOT RECORDED.

After the outbreak of hostilities in 1939, American polo players soon realised that things were not ever going to be the same again. Aware that international competition was out of the question, the number of chukkas in the 1940 US Open was reduced to six in order to encourage lower handicapped players. Sympathy for the plight of Britain and her Allies was great and a benefit match for the "Bundles for Britain" fund attracted huge crowds to Washington, DC, to watch an exhibition match between Texas and Meadow Brook. This feast of superlative polo was the last really top-class event that was to be seen in America until the end of the war.

As in World War I, polo was to lose many of its best and most promising players – the most prominent amongst these being Tommy Hitchcock Jr. By cruel irony he died at the controls of a P-51 Mustang fighter plane as it crashed on Salisbury Plain in England in 1944. Dying in action at speed while controlling a Mustang seemed to some a fitting – if tragic – way for this greatest of horsemen and polo players to bow out.

Argentina was little involved in the war that was ravaging the whole of Europe, and – whilst others were disastrously distracted – they used this time to good effect. Ranch life was thriving and with it young Argentinian players were being given every encouragement to improve their skills on a large number of excellent ponies. The dramatic effects of this were to be seen by all those returning to the game at the end of hostilities.

Meanwhile, for many the future looked too bleak to contemplate. In England some of the major playing fields had been dug up and used for growing vegetables, or as public recreation grounds. This was especially the state of affairs in and around London. Once the mainstay of British polo, the Army was helping to win a war, and it was widely predicted that the changes wrought by these black times would forever kill the game. Thankfully, however, the war also encouraged strong men to be resourceful and with polo in their blood, some were determined not to see the sport die.

Soon after the end of hostilities, at Ham on the edge of London in one of the Royal parks, Billy Walsh and Cyril Harrison revived play at a little club which had been founded in 1931. Elsewhere chukkas were also beginning at clubs throughout the south of England – most of which did not survive for long. In the 1940s Arthur Lucas, head of the polo playing dynasty which now includes international players of note, had started the Woolmers Park club at his home in Hertfordshire. Quietly things were moving but the standard of play was not particularly high. However, important people were encouraged by developments. The old Cheshire Club, begun in 1872, was restored in 1951 and the following year the Earl Bathurst and his brother revived the Cirencester Park Polo Club in the grounds of their family home. Nearby in Oxfordshire, the Kirtlington Park club was reopened by Alan Budgett in 1954.

The most important club in the immediate post-war

years was at Cowdray Park in West Sussex. Viscount Cowdray – a 4-goal player in 1939 – inherited the title and estate in 1933 on the death of his father; who had been chairman of the Hurlingham Polo Association. During the war he lost his left arm but that did not stop him from pursuing his favourite sport. When peace came, with the help of his stud groom William Woodcock, he maintained an impressive string of 50 ponies which he played regularly on the old club fields. He continued to play until the 1960s, using a hook to hold the reins. Always generous and thoughtful, Lord Cowdray was a great encourager of young players, lending his horses free to officer cadets from the Royal Military Academy at Sandhurst.

At this time, exchanges were taking place with Argentina and men who had worked hard to restore the standard of their play met with such players as Jack Nelson, Louis Lacey, Juan Carlos Harriott and the three Lalors. For England men such as John Lakin (Lord Cowdray's brother-in-law), Lt.Col. Humphrey Guinness, John Traill Jr., Bob Skene and Lt.Col. Peter Dollar were finding something of their old form. A newcomer to the game was HRH Prince Philip who had started to play in Malta in 1950. He played regularly for Lord Cowdray's team and naturally enough was supported by his family. Thus crowds of spectators flocked to Sussex – more in the hope of seeing members of the Royal Family than the polo. In 1953, more than 12,000 people attended the Coronation Cup matches played at Cowdray Park in Midhurst to honour the coronation of Her Majesty the Queen.

England had beaten a team from Argentina in 1951, but in a 1953 series, when there was a tournament for six national teams (including Chile, which was coming to the fore on the polo field), Argentina beat England in the final. Many of the great pre-war players took part, the team from Meadow Brook consisting of Americans Pete Bostwick, Philip Iglehart, Dicky Santamarina and Dev Milburn Jr. Representing England were Lt.Col. Alec Harper, Gerald Balding, Humphrey Guinness and John Lakin. The victors from Argentina were Alex Mihanovich, Eduardo Braun-Mendez, Ernesto Lalor and Juan Carlos Alberdi. The huge crowd saw some marvellous polo and the games were watched by the Queen, the Duke of Edinburgh and Princess Margaret, who had several friends who played the game.

At last polo in England seemed on its way back to its former glory. Royal interest helped bring in the spectators, who in their turn helped to pay some of the enormous bills which maintenance of the sport required. In 1955 the Duke of Edinburgh, by now a 5-goal player, helped establish a new club based on the Household Brigade in the near-perfect setting of Windsor Great Park. The seven regiments of the Brigade all have a special relationship with the monarch, who is Colonel-in-Chief of them all. The home park of the Queen's Windsor Castle was a natural site for the club and thus the Guards Polo Club (originally named the Household Brigade Polo Club) came into being. It was soon to become the largest in Europe and attracted much international interest. In 1960 the Queen's Cup was presented by Her Majesty to be played for in the club by high-goal teams as the first important series of games at the beginning of the English season.

After the war, the headquarters of British polo, not unnaturally, became sited at Midhurst. In 1956 the first British Open Championship for the Cowdray Park Gold Cup was played, and as the premier tournament it has been played for continuously since then, attracting most of the high-goal teams playing in England during each season.

Through the 1960s and 1970s in Britain there was a steady rise in interest in polo. Pony Club polo for the young was soon attracting dozens of teams and beginning to provide young players – who eventually were to gain international reputations. Services polo also had a steadily rising following, thanks especially to the facilities provided at the Guards club and Lord Mountbatten's considerable interest and encouragement. Lord Louis' book, *An Introduction to Polo*, first published in 1931 under the pseudonym of "Marco", was perennially popular with all generations and ran through several printings.

Far left LORD COWDRAY ACKNOWLEDGES A FRIEND BETWEEN CHUKKAS AT HIS HOME CLUB WHERE HE HAS DONE SO MUCH FOR THE GAME. *Above* A TRIUMPHANT ARGENTINE TEAM WITH THE CORONATION CUP AFTER THEY HAD BEATEN ENGLAND IN 1953.

In post-war independent India it took some time before confidence to revive official polo was strong enough. However, in Calcutta contributions had been sought from a number of distinguished local people and the old practice ground at Ellenborough was brought to playing condition, even though the field was not ideal as the western sideline had to wend its way around a venerable old tree. The first post-war exhibition match was played in December 1951 beween a Cooch Behar team and one from the club. The Maharaja of Jaipur generously donated six ponies and the club was thus able to maintain its position as the oldest surviving polo centre in the world. Five years later it moved back to its former grounds in the centre of the Calcutta racecourse.

Political changes on the Indian sub-continent were rapid and the game inevitably suffered. The departure of the British, the changing social status of the ruling families, and the upheavals caused by Partition had all taken their toll. However, a proud tradition was maintained and many international visitors were attracted to India to play polo. Prince Philip played with an international team on the occasion of the centenary of the Calcutta club and many others were able to enjoy the hospitality of patrons in this and other polo centres that soon grew up.

The famous Jaipur team, which pre-war had enjoyed such a winning reputation in both England and India, played again in Jaipur and at the clubs that were reforming to play the sport throughout the country: Delhi, Bombay, Bangalore, Meerut and Hyderabad. With Hanut Singh, H H Jaipur won the Indian Polo Association Championship on six occasions from 1956 to 1961, thus ensuring that his team took home the trophy no less than 15 consecutive times. His Highness had dominated the game for some years before the war and afterwards he was to make his presence felt wherever polo was played.

During the 1960s in India the army began to dominate the game, having better resources for ponies, particularly within the 61st Cavalry, the world's last remaining active horse-mounted regiment. Gradually, however, the interest of the maharajas waned and the game went into another decline in the place of its rebirth. More recently, increased civilian involvement has helped to keep the sport alive and polo moves from centre to centre throughout the year.

Above THE WINNERS AND RUNNERS-UP OF THE 1939 PRINCE OF WALES CUP FINALS IN DELHI: LEFT TO RIGHT: R.B. MAN SINGH, KANWAR JABBAR SINGH, HH THE MAHARAJA OF JAIPUR, RAJ KUMAR PRITHI SINGH, RAO RAJAH HANUT SINGH, CAPT. KUMAR AMAR SINGH, RAO RAJAH ABHAY SINGH AND CAPT. MCCONNEL.

The "dehorsification" of the American army after World War II was also to have a great effect on polo in the USA, the game losing one of its most important support systems when effectively army polo was scrapped. Although many civilians were able to buy up the horses being sold off by the army – which helped considerably – as in other countries it was left to a few enthusiasts to revive the playing of the game. The National Open Championship was revived in 1946 and was won by a team from Mexico. Foreign competition was from now on going to be of considerable influence and in many ways was to ensure the continuance of top-rate polo in America.

The advent of television in a majority of US homes led to an increase in the numbers of armchair sportsmen who were happy to watch their chosen sports being performed by professionals. Cecil Smith became the focal point of this group in polo and in 1949 Pete Bostwick, long an innovator, held the first all-professional tournament on his field in New York. Ten teams played over a period of two weeks for a prize purse of $5,000 put up by Bostwick. The eventual winners were Del Carroll, Al Parsalls, Buddy Combs and George Oliver, and prize money was more than covered by the gate receipts.

The 1950s were not a time when the American public took much interest in the game but new young players were developing their skills. In the early 1950s the home of United States polo, Meadow Brook, was sold for development and Paul Butler's Oak Brook Polo Club, just outside Chicago, which was founded in 1922, was to become the focal point of polo in America. The 1954 National Open was played at Oak Brook and the four teams which took part contained names from both the old and the new sections of the game: Pete Bostwick, Cecil Smith, Michael Phipps, Harold Barry, Bill Barry, Del Carroll, and Ray Harrington Jr. By the time the mantle had moved on to the new generation of high-goal players, the US Polo Association had moved its headquarters to Chicago and in the late 1960s that group were taking positions of responsibility.

In the Southern states polo was enjoying continuous growth with games being held in the Miami Orange Bowl every Friday night during the first three months of the year. Thirty ponies were maintained – thanks to the gate money

Above HM THE QUEEN WITH JOHN MAXWELL OF THE WESTBURY HOTEL IN 1970 FOLLOWING THE GAME BETWEEN PRINCE PHILIP'S WINDSOR PARK TEAM AND JACK OXLEY'S BOCA RATON FROM AMERICA.

received from the enormous crowds of spectators who flocked to see top players from all over the country competing against the local side. Games were played by collegiate teams from the University of Miami and visitors from Yale, Harvard and other polo-playing centres of learning. The excellent winter climate also encouraged others to set up clubs in Florida, such as the Gulfstream club and the Boca Raton club nearby. In the early 1970s William T. Ylvisaker began working on the setting up of the Palm Beach Polo and Country Club, which was to attract most of the world's best players.

Between 1950 and 1980, well over 100 new clubs registered with the USPA. In the 1950s, Ohio, Pennsylvania, Alberta, Oklahoma and California gained clubs; in the 1960s Wyoming, Texas and Virginia were among those who founded new polo facilities; in the 1970s, Louisiana, Washington, New Jersey, Tennessee, Massachusetts and Mississippi all experienced the founding of clubs; in the 1980s the growth continued with such states as Connecticut, Maine, Iowa, North and South Carolina, Colorado and Vermont all enjoying new clubs. Most were small but all contributed to a steady growth in the popularity of the game. A welcome development came

in 1967 when Bill Ylvisaker set up the Polo Training Foundation for the teaching and improving of the sport.

As in England, the interest of the "First Family" in horses did much to encourage a renewed public awareness of polo. A 1961 tour of Pakistan by the President's wife, Jackie Kennedy, included a stunt thought up by the State Department in which a polo team from America met one from the Pakistan Army at the Lahore National Horse and Cattle Show. Describing the event the editor of *Polo* magazine wrote: "It was a triumph of diplomacy, if not of American polo. The Americans had played well enough to make the finals, but not quite well enough to win. If the State Department had written the script it could not have come out better." The tour was repeated in 1964 and in 1969 and again proved a great success, causing one local general to remark that the polo visitors did "a lot more good than these long-haired violinists they keep sending out here . . ."

Above THE 1971 CORONATION CUP, WON BY AMERICA, WAS THE FIRST INTERNATIONAL BETWEEN THE USA AND THE UK FOR 35 YEARS.
Right THE LATE EDDIE MOORE. HIS 10-GOAL PERFORMANCE WAS AN INSPIRATION TO THOSE PLAYING IN BRITAIN DURING THE 1970S.

After the war, international polo moved in fits and starts. In 1950 a team flew from America to Buenos Aires to contest the Copa de las Americas. They took with them ten ponies and their hosts lent a further 16. These were selected by the American team of Peter Perkins, George Oliver, Lewis Smith and Pete Bostwick, who were also taking part in that year's Argentine Open. They did well enough to reach the final but lost to the Venado Tuerto team. For the Cup of the Americas, Bostwick was replaced by Del Carroll, making a 31-goal team. Argentina fielded the Venado Tuerto 37-goal side of Juan and Roberto Cavanagh and Enrique and Juan Carlos Alberdi. The splendid team play of the Argentinians ensured their victory in two matches but the Americans put up a hard fight and were far from disgraced.

The Copa de las Americas was not played for again until 1966. With the score for the previous series standing at 2-2, the Americans selected their team from a pool of players with handicaps of seven and above. The trip to Buenos Aires was supported by many generous patrons who lent horses and it was decided also to contest the World 30-goal Championship. Northrup Knox led a strong squad but both series of games were eventually won by the Argentinians who fielded Gaston and Francisco Dorignac, Horacio Heguy and Juan Carlos Harriott. The 40,000 spectators were generous in their praise of the Americans – even if they did not expect them to win. In 1969 the same Argentinian team beat off another strong American challenge.

Many of America's top players, such as the 10-goalers Robert Skene and Tommy Wayman, travelled internationally, as did lesser players in lower handicapped teams. The days when ponies could be transported easily and cheaply were gradually dying out but polo hospitality and the cosmopolitan nature of its history ensured that there was always a welcome wherever the game was played and local ponies could be provided.

England began formal international challenge matches in 1971 when, with a sizeable number of top-class Americans playing in the country, the Hurlingham Polo Association challenged the USA to play for the Coronation Cup. The game took place at Cowdray Park and was fought between, for America, Ronnie Tongg, Bill Linfoot, Harold and Joe Barry and, for England, the Hon. Mark Vestey, Paul Withers and brothers Julian and Howard Hipwood. Four thousand spectators attended, led by the

Prince of Wales – who had begun playing polo in 1964 – and Lord Louis Mountbatten. The Duke of Edinburgh was one of the umpires. America won the game 9-6 and so another challenge was issued for the following year.

That 1972 challenge took place at the Guards Club in Windsor Great Park and attracted even larger crowds – a trend for this international match which has continued until today. To the senior game was added one between two under-25 sides which included Prince Charles. Again the Americans, this time with Corky Linfoot replacing an injured Tongg and Roy Barry Jr. in place of Joe Barry, beat the English who fielded the Hipwoods, Lord Patrick Beresford (who replaced the injured Withers), and Major Ronnie Ferguson. In the Young England-America game, Red Armour scored the winning goal in the final chukka after an exciting competition.

Defeat for England followed in the next two years when Bill Ylvisaker and Tommy Wayman played for the United States. In 1975 the Americans decided not to submit a representative team and a side from South America was invited to contest the Coronation Cup. Four Argentinians – who were already playing for various English teams – comprised the opposition who met the Hipwoods, Withers and M. Hare. Juan José Alberdi was joined by Eddie Moore, Hector Barrantes and the young 3-goaler Gonzalo Pieres, and together they defeated the England side. This English defeat was to recur for another three years until England beat a side from Mexico in 1979. Each year various teams are put together to compete against England in a high-goal show game, the gate receipts benefiting polo throughout the country. England continues to have a mixed record in these matches but the July International Day still provides the main opportunity for national representative polo in Britain.

The extraordinary conflict over the Falkland Islands between Britain and Argentina – which began in April 1982 – led to the banning of Argentinian players from official games in England. This serious prohibition was to affect English polo considerably as it threw the high-goal teams back on to native and Commonwealth talent before an influx of other South Americans, particularly the Mexicans, arrived. Many thought the ban made the English game stronger and certainly at its inception it seemed to do little harm. The ban continued but finally, following the symbolic gesture of an important Argentinian team – led by Francisco Dorignac, President of the Argentine Polo Association – playing a practice game with the England team in the week before the international Hurlingham Polo Association match against North America in 1988, it has been lifted.

In 1974 the Camacho Cup was revived for America's international competition against Mexico. The Americans won in that year and again in 1975, but the following year, when the Gracida family became involved, they were beaten, as they were in 1981. Guillermo Gracida was by now leading a formidable family team, including his sons Memo and Carlos and nephew Ruben, who were to become welcome additions to teams both in America and England as well as in their home country.

THE AMERICAN WINNERS OF THE 1946 CAMACHO CUP WHEN THE UNITED STATES TEAM BEAT MEXICO AT MEADOW BROOK: MIKE PHIPPS, CECIL SMITH, STEWART IGLEHART AND PETER PERKINS.

As the numbers playing and watching polo all over the world increased, so did the interest of big business and in the 1970s the commercial possibilities of polo began to be recognised by corporate sponsors. As a vehicle for reaching a particularly well-disposed section of society the polo match had few equals for the selling of "up-market" products – or for the entertaining of clients with the power to forge expensive deals. Many of those who were starting to play the game had already made their mark in their own professional field and were thus able to introduce important supporters whose sponsorship money in turn reduced their own outlay on the sport.

Into the last two decades of the twentieth century, the international aspects of the game are increasingly being emphasised and because of this the desire for a world championship has been expressed. Bill Ylvisaker inaugurated an annual event for teams with a rating of 25 goals or more and offered substantial prize money. It was dubbed "The World Cup" and was perhaps the nearest to that concept yet achieved. Most of the highest handicapped world players attended and, apart from the Argentine Open, the games have provided some of the

world's best polo. The formation of an International Federation of Polo – still to be recognised by the British HPA – is making great strides and offers the best opportunity so far for a real world cup series.

Since World War II, the steady growth experienced within the game of polo has been remarkable by any standards. The United States Polo Association, which moved its headquarters to Kentucky in 1986, has nearly 200 affiliated clubs, which include school and college centres, and represents more than 2,000 listed players. In Britain the Hurlingham Polo Association governs 24 clubs with 17 affiliated overseas associations. Some 850 players are listed with a recognised handicap and, as in other countries, this does not take into account those learning the game. The Argentine Polo Association is perhaps the biggest in the world with more than 150 clubs and a combined strength of at least 5,000 handicapped players.

As the year 2000 approaches, the game is achieving new heights and names from the 1960s, 1970s and 1980s that appear in polo's recorded history can be sung as heroes as much as any from the past. One thing is certain: polo has an honourable past – but also a glittering future.

THE RAJMATA OF JAIPUR

THE PEOPLE OF INDIA are a nation of great horsemen and horsewomen. And none glitters more brightly in her emerald green sari than polo's most glamorous "groupie" – the Rajmata of Jaipur. She's seen these days on her self-appointed polo rounds from her native playing fields of Rajasthan and England's Windsor Park to the US high-goal haunts of Oak Brook, Ill., Greenwich, Conn., Palm Beach Polo and Country Club, Florida, and the new home of the USPA's US Open in Lexington, Kentucky.

Dreams have had a lot to do with her current polo presence. They were polarised for her as a child by a 22-year-old polo demigod. "My dear," says Gayatri Devi, the Rajmata, "my dream was always that one day I'd grow up to be his groom." She sweeps back a wing of raven hair; the Jaipur-green sari flutters; the patrician stare relents; the musical voice turns mischievous. "But I never became his groom. I became his wife instead."

He, of course, was His Highness Maharaja Man Singh of Jaipur, statesman, soldier and captain of the legendary Jaipur Team, the "Fearsome Foursome" that in 1933 swept every high-goal tournament on the English circuit: the Hurlingham Open, the Coronation Cup, the Indian Empire Shield, the Roehampton Open and the Ranelagh Open.

"When they returned to India, I was 13 years old," recalls the Rajmata, "and my mother the Maharani of Cooch Behar invited the Maharaja of Jaipur to our home. He became a sort of hero in our household, and so my romance with polo began when I was very young." In those days, her "Jai" maintained a private army, had a string of some 120 top polo ponies, and chose his polo teams from among his own friends, a proud cavalry regiment and a superbly mounted personal bodyguard. "I saw my first game at the age of four," she says; "every child in Jaipur knew the game of polo."

The Rajmata's romance ultimately became a six-year courtship culminating in a wedding that made the *Guinness Book of Records* as the most extravagant the world had ever seen. Meanwhile, the ruler of India's fabled Pink City continued to make the kind of polo history that wedded his glamorous young wife forever to the Game of Kings. Jai's great Jaipur Team, recalls the Rajmata, consisted of Maharaja Man Singh (9 goals) at Back, Rao Raja Hanut Singh (9 goals) at number 3, Rao Raja Abbey Singh (8 goals) at number 2, and Maharaj Pridhi Singh (8-goals) at number 1. This 34-goal juggernaut surely would have made good its 1933 challenge to America had not World War II intervened.

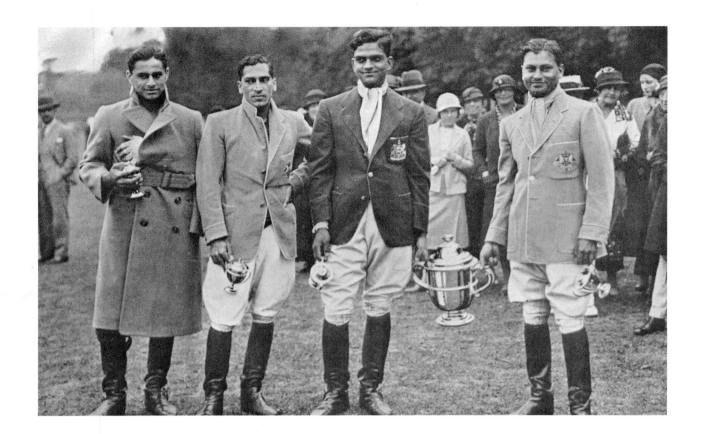

THE RAJMATA WAS ABLE TO ENJOY THE SUCCESS OF HER HUSBAND'S TEAM
DURING HIS MANY VISITS TO ENGLAND. THE JAIPUR TEAM IS PICTURED
HERE AFTER WINNING THE RANELAGH OPEN CUP.

In Jaipur's golden age of polo – from the thirties well into the fifties – crowds of over 100,000 would throng to Jaipur Field at Rambagh Palace, and even in Calcutta. "It was a superb spectacle," says the Rajmata. "Jaipur colours were green, and so we'd attend all in green saris. It was a big romance, this polo thing." *Vogue* magazine's Diana Vreeland once said: "Pink is the navy blue of India." To paraphrase that fashion doyenne on behalf of the Rajmata: "Green is the royal hue of Jaipur polo."

Back in European contention in 1957, the all-India team, captained by His Highness Maharaja Man Singh, swept all competition to win the World Cup Polo Tournament at Deauville, France. In India during those years, as her "Jai" and his team rode from polo crown to crown, his young wife – who was herself an accomplished horsewoman – began to find the game itself irresistible. "I started to stick and ball with Lady Mountbatten whose husband was then Viceroy of India," she says. But when she presumed to suggest a ladies' team that might play on the hallowed Jaipur "Chaugen", or playing field, the sternly adoring husband said: "No woman is ever going to play on the Jaipur polo grounds."

Above THE RAJMATA PRESENTS A TROPHY TO HRH THE PRINCE OF WALES.
Below THE RAJMATA IS A WELCOME VISITOR TO POLO CLUBS THROUGHOUT
THE WORLD. HERE SHE IS SEEN WITH MARCOS URANGA, PRESIDENT OF THE
INTERNATIONAL POLO FEDERATION, AND MRS PHILIP IGLEHART AT LEXINGTON.

Polo: JAIPUR EASY WINNERS OF THE CORONATION CUP

THE KING AND QUEEN AT RANELAGH

The King and Queen on Saturday honoured the Ranelagh Club with a visit, and witnessed the final of the King's Coronation Cup tournament. After the match, in which Jaipur beat the Royal Scots Greys by nine goals to five, the Queen presented the cup to the Maharaja of Jaipur.

ANOTHER JAIPUR SUCCESS

KING'S CORONATION CUP

ROYAL SCOTS GREYS OUTPLAYED

JAIPUR'S year is the obvious way of describing the London polo season of 1933. In years to come it will most assuredly be referred to as such—never before has a team made so clean a sweep of our open tournaments. It is a waste of time to try and imagine what would have happened had the Hurricanes or El Gordo—two famous teams of recent years—still been in existence.

We do not agree with some of our contemporaries, who hail Jaipur as the best team ever seen, nor do we consider them invincible. We feel confident they would not have continued their triumphant career had they been persuaded to go to America, nevertheless whatever their capabilities or limitations, the fact remains that we have been this year unable to produce a team to press and test them. They have been seen at their best against Someries House in the Champion Cup, and in the first two chukkers in the Coron-

JAIPUR'S FOURTH CUP

The King and Queen Watch Victorious Indians

SOME REAL POLO

POLO JOTTINGS

THE INDIAN TEAM'S FINE FORM

Third Championship for Jaipur

JAIPUR'S BRILLIANT TOUR.

POLO CHAMPIONS AT DUNSTER

WEST SOMERSET POLO CLUB.

Fine Play by the Jaipur Team.

Maharajah of Jaipur's Famous Team Provide Unprecedented Attraction

WINNERS OF OPEN CHALLENGE CUP.

BRILLIANT GAMES AND PICTURESQUE PONY PARADES

THE JAIPUR SCRAPBOOKS TELL OF THE SUCCESS OF THE MAHARAJA'S TEAM.

Mild matrimonial comeuppance occurred a few years later, recalls the Rajmata during a polo season at Cowdray Park where the Maharaja with Lord Cowdray was helping rejuvenate the game in post-war England. "In his first tournament at Cowdray," she says, "Jai's Number 1 was a lady, Lord Cowdray's sister; and the opposing Number 1 was a second Cowdray sister." The Rajmata dared ask after the game: "Aha, I thought women were not permitted . . ." Jai's response is unrecorded.

Although thoroughly committed to polo and its regal lifestyle both in Jaipur and *en voyage*, the Rajmata began to play a leading role in Indian politics in 1962. And there were occasional marital ride-offs, she recalls, as politics and polo campaigns vied for attention. For instance, she, on having to refuse an evening gala because of Jai's polo next day: "My life is being ruled – and overruled – by polo and politics!" He: "You know, my dear, there are a lot of politics in polo!"

Even though His Highness Man Singh had conferred his vast and powerful kingdom upon free India in 1951, polo as he and his wife had always known it continued to dominate their lives with its fierce joys. Then, in 1970, tragedy struck. The man who once asked his betrothed as they drove secretly in his Bentley through London's Hyde Park whether she'd still care for him were he injured playing polo, died in a tournament on 24 June 1970 at Cirencester Park, England.

"People wonder why I still watch the game," says the Rajmata. "It's the game I love; I like seeing it grow; watching the new developments. And as I watch, my life with Jai in polo comes back to me with all its beauty, the perfection of its horsemanship, the triumph of its teamwork. There never was anything like his Jaipur Team."

Today, she celebrates the perpetuation of the dash and class of that polo world by presenting cups at two top polo events – at the Oak Brook Polo Club outside Chicago, whose founder Paul Butler first hosted the royal Jaipur couple in the 1950s, and at Windsor Park in England. The former occurs in late September, the latter in late June, and the lady herself is faithfully on hand to bestow these memorial trophies to up-and-coming players of whom Jai himself would have been most proud. He inaugurated both cups back in 1968. The 1988 Jaipur Cup at Oak Brook, as traditionally when she arrives, invoked its own monsoon. "Lately," she says, "it's been suggested to Oak Brook Polo Club chairman Michael Butler that he be paid to keep me away!" To a player, of course, Oak Brook poloists have refused and in 1988 the Rajmata awarded her coveted cup to the White Ash Team who triumphed over Lithographics with the help of Paul Butler's granddaughter Reutie Butler, much to the delight of that genteel polo feminist the Rajmata.

Late in September 1988, the Rajmata made another flying US polo visit to Lexington, Kentucky, where in sunlight as brilliant as Rajasthan's – but cooler – she observed the first-ever US Open in its official new USPA headquarters. For the Rajmata, the hard-won triumph of Guy Wildenstein's Diables Bleus team over S. K. Johnston III's Coca-Cola squad epitomised the evolving style of US high-goal polo, a blend of knightly grace, cavalry furore and rodeo freestyle.

"Sponsorship and professionalism today, especially in America," she says, "have made all the difference. Without them modern polo just wouldn't survive. Pity we can't seem to attract sponsorship in India where polo as I knew it is on the wane."

Indian polo today is still vigorous and draws its high-goalers from the country's single remaining cavalry regiment and the President's Body Guard as the September–March season sweeps from Jaipur south to Madras and thence north to Calcutta and New Delhi. And even as in America, says the Rajmata, some major Indian games are televised and crowds of 20,000 still turn up to watch a game if a big personality is on hand.

This high-flying polo devotee may yet contribute to a polo renaissance in the ancestral home of her 2,500-year-old sport. "At my small stud farm in India," she says, "I'm now breeding pure Indian horses, some from the lines my husband wanted to use for polo ponies. They're mainly for show." But one day soon, perhaps, the Rajmata may be raising polo ponies . . .

A THIRD GENERATION PLAYER, FRANCE'S LIONEL MACAIRE SHARES
HIS COUNTRY'S TOP HANDICAP WITH HIS BROTHER STEFAN.

3

PLAYING TODAY

The thrill and excitement generated by playing polo is spreading daily across the world as players and clubs proliferate from country to country. And at every level – especially in the United States of America and England – there are more teams competing than ever before.

Argentina still continues to dominate polo, providing at least half the world's players and enjoying a very high standard of play throughout the country. There are many reasons for this dominance, perhaps the primary one being the early start made by most of the children. The Mexicans have an abundance of good performers for relatively few players and all the other South American countries play polo to a high standard – but none of them approaching the numbers and proficiency achieved by Argentina.

The British colonial legacy lives on, partly in the fact that every country that was once in the British Commonwealth still has an interest in the game, but most of them in a small way. For example, a country which has a high average of good players is New Zealand where fast and furious farm polo is enjoyed by the sort of people who in other countries believe that polo is out of their financial reach.

Before World War II, the British augmented their numbers of high-goal players with Army officers from cavalry regiments who had vastly improved their skill and handicaps while serving in India. They became known as the "hired assassins" – although the most they accepted from the polo patrons of the day was hospitality together with a few perks. Today the professional has inherited the mantle of "hired assassin" and fulfils it most aptly when for the first time he arrives from a foreign country as an unknown and better than his handicap.

Contrary to what many believe, no one in Argentina will actually play professionally for money, and even the few grooms who play there do so for sheer enjoyment only. However, as professionals in foreign parts, Argentinians can and do ask for large payments, although many in lieu of a fee accept expenses – plus a price guaranteed for the ponies which come with them. During the ban on Argentinian players in England, a growing number of New Zealand and Australian professionals – many coming from farming backgrounds – have considerably augmented their incomes.

In the USA and England the "total professional" has been operating for some time. In the States, many belong to dynasties that have passed the profession from father to son over two or three generations and these men will be found playing somewhere on the North American continent throughout the year. However, some of them like to devote a month or more to training young ponies, either for sale or as replacements for those sold from their regular string. Sadly, there are those professionals who can never fulfil their full potential because they always have to sell their best ponies at times when as players they most need them.

It is easier for visitors without home-base expenses and taxes to offer their services at attractive rates and there has been considerable concern expressed in the USA about the proliferation of Argentinian professionals playing at the expense of the home-grown variety who cannot find employment. A similar problem in England has previously been solved by bringing in a rule that limits the number of foreign players in each team, but as polo becomes more popular in the US there is every possibility that the opportunity of employment will increase sufficiently to deal with this problem without bringing in restrictions.

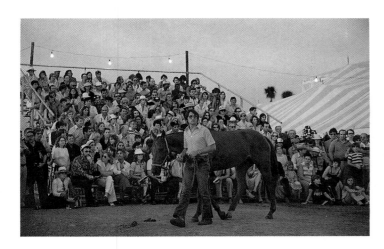

Nowadays, the sight of four good amateurs banding together to form a team and sharing the costs equally is a rare phenomenon. This is because the majority of teams contain one or more professionals and their "employer" – the patron – an amateur who is convinced that he cannot achieve results without putting himself totally in the hands of a professional who will both coach him and help him to acquit himself well in matches. Unfortunately, this often results in a situation in which the patron is precluded from taking a major role because he leaves everything to the professional. The patron has little opportunity of getting better, although he may play many matches in one year. An increase in confidence goes hand in hand with improvement, but if a patron is not trusted to play a significant role, how can he become a better player?

There is a growing opinion in the polo world that this situation could be remedied with the introduction of an effective team coach. It is felt that not only would the extra contribution extracted by the coach from the patron add to the team's performance, but the professional would be able to fulfil his own role more effectively. Furthermore, the overall standard of all players – including that of the professionals – would be raised considerably.

Another reason put forward for the use of a coach is that players themselves would be learning something about the art of coaching, thus paving the way for their own continued involvement in polo when the day came when they would be too old to play. Furthermore, many people believe that a good coach would remove much of the acrimony that exists between team members when things go wrong. Instead of blaming each other, constructive criticism from the coach would avoid unpleasantness and enhance future performance.

The human ego varies enormously but in polo some patrons seem to fall into the same trap. They firmly believe that they will be admired by their peers for achieving a place on the field in a high-goal polo match alongside some of the best players in the world. However, sometimes the result is the very opposite with patrons becoming the objects of ridicule to knowledgeable spectators. The high-goal player is such an athlete and artist that the performance of those of lesser ability will pale into insignificance alongside his. But, it is thought, if team strategy was always planned by a coach who co-ordinated from the sideline, then weaker players could be encouraged to participate more effectively. With a non-playing coach, the patron would get far more out of the game while developing into a much better player.

The Argentine Polo Association has no need to introduce a coaching system whilst their country's position in the polo world is supreme. But more polo people are being convinced that any country wishing to challenge the Argentinian hegemony cannot hope to do so without throwing tradition to the winds and setting up a system of in-depth instruction at all levels of the game.

Above left KEEN INTEREST IS SHOWN DURING THE REGULAR SALES OF POLO PONIES - OFTEN SOLD AFTER THEY HAVE JUST BEEN SEEN IN ACTION DURING A MATCH. *Right* WILLIAM YLVISAKER, A HIGH GOAL PATRON AND AN HONORARY GOVERNOR OF THE USPA.

Methods – and degrees of success – of polo instruction vary from country to country, but as a general rule it is usually limited to beginners and low-goal players who have not attained a rating above a zero handicap. In the USA the Polo Association has set up a training foundation which organises annual six-week polo clinics at the University of Virginia. These are run by a Rege Ludwig who, like many others, believes in the crucial importance of riding and places priority on this throughout his clinic. He is a successful polo pony trainer who, at his home in Texas, brings on ponies to order for many clients. Rege also travels extensively to instruct at polo clubs throughout the States and has recently set-up a winter base at Palm Springs, California.

Surprisingly, there are few other effective polo instructors in the USA. The gap between high- and low-goal polo is enormous and the best players are so far ahead of the rest that it is difficult for them to relate to many of the problems encountered at the lower levels. Hence instructing is undertaken only by a few unselfish and dedicated people, such as the Californian 8-goaler Joel Baker, who is the highest handicap player to do this. He often works together with his wife, Oatsy, who is one of the best women polo players in America.

In England the New Zealander Peter Grace at his Rangitiki Polo School has established himself as the principal instructor for the British (along with Somerville Livingstone Learnmouth at the Guards club and others at Cirencester Park) and has played an important and significant part in introducing many people to polo. He emphasises the importance of effective striking and his clients start by standing on chairs to learn the basic striking techniques, then move on to stick and ball work on ponies before progressing directly to actual chukkas. His daughters – the "Four Graces" – are not only useful players themselves, but add an attractive and most helpful support to their father's teaching.

At Whitfield Court in Waterford, Ireland, Major Hugh Dawnay is currently in his 13th year of giving polo instruction based on his own unique system. He formulated this while serving in the British Army in Germany and recognises that a successful future for polo depends on organised instruction with good continuity at every level. He teaches that all-round vision on the polo field enables good tactics to become a reality. From this, riding is made relatively easy because confusion will be reduced and a pony will want to follow the rider who clearly executes a strategy. Although he places priority and emphasis on tactics, he tackles the basic areas – tactics,

riding and striking – separately and covers each in detail.

A day of instruction at Hugh Dawnay's school is divided into seven distinct parts: training on the wooden horse; improving riding ability at the riding school; tactics lecture using a model table; working on a mini ground where set-piece tactics can be walked through; developing stick and ball techniques with ponies on the full-size polo ground; practice chukkas; and finally a video-assisted critique in which all aspects of the pupils' performance are discussed and analysed. The course is designed to give the novice total immersion into polo and Hugh Dawnay claims that it will bring a person to a level which a new player attains only after two years playing normal club polo.

Below THE WOODEN HORSE HAS LONG BEEN A TRIED AND TESTED AID TO POLO INSTRUCTION.

Above WHITFIELD COURT POLO SCHOOL IN IRELAND WHERE PUPILS
ARE TAUGHT TACTICS ON FOOT (***centre***) AND ON THE TABLE TOP
(***below***) BY MAJOR HUGH DAWNAY.

In recent years more and more Argentinians have started polo instruction on their *estancias*. This trend was led by the late Eduardo Moore and then followed by La Martina and many nationalities have enjoyed hospitality in beautiful surroundings – besides participating daily in stick and ball and chukkas. However, wherever one plays in Argentina, one profits from experiencing a speed and flair that is unique to this country. Initially, the foreign novice will feel lost but inevitably valuable lessons will be absorbed. It is a sad fact that the English ban on Argentinians after the Falklands conflict has meant that many players have missed this important influence, and that their polo progression has thus been delayed.

Casa de Campo in the Dominican Republic is a wonderful facility enjoyed by many travelling polo enthusiasts. There an incredible number of ponies give a wide variety of mounts while enthusiastic grooms are always available to complete a team. The current polo manager is Brigadier Arthur Douglas-Nugent, who in his younger days contributed enormously to British Army polo.

It would be difficult for anyone outside South America to organise anything equivalent to the experience of children of adult players in Argentina. Almost before they can walk they are riding little ponies bare back around the *estancias*. Then – in some cases before reaching 10 years old – they graduate to the full-size pony to practise stick and ball. From this, hand/eye co-ordination becomes instinctive and by their early teens they are participating in chukkas at an incredibly high standard of play.

Many people believe that something similar to the Argentine childhood experience should be attempted in other countries – especially in Britain and the US. Britain has a very good Pony Club polo organisation and excellent tournaments, with large entries, take place every summer. But the children are not given enough practice and have little or no opportunity to experience anything approaching their Argentinian counterparts. Furthermore, for many an abrupt end of the road confronts them when their Pony Club days are over. A few lucky ones receive scholarships to New Zealand and benefit considerably. Before the Falklands War, several even luckier young men went to Argentina during the winter and these support the middle of the English handicap, where they may feel themselves to be a little isolated. Millfield is the only known British school to include polo in its curriculum. In the US, many colleges play indoor polo, coaching is constructive and in the annual championships a good standard is reached. Yet, many participants drop polo after leaving college – and those who do continue have to start virtually from scratch to learn the outdoor game.

THE NEED FOR GOOD BALANCE AND AN EYE FOR THE BALL IS WELL DEMONSTRATED BY 10-GOALER EDDIE MOORE.

Left YOUNG PLAYERS IN THE ARGENTINE ARE ABLE TO REACH EXTRAORDINARILY HIGH STANDARDS THANKS TO THE SYSTEM WHICH PUTS THEM ON GOOD PONIES TO PLAY FAST CHUKKAS WITH THEIR PEERS EARLY IN THEIR PLAYING CAREERS. THERE IS NO LACK OF CONFIDENCE AMONGST THESE BOYS.

Right MANY DISTINGUISHED OLD PLAYERS GIVE THEIR TIME TO INSTRUCT THE YOUNG. MAHARAJ PREM SINGH WAS A TOP INDIAN INTERNATIONAL PLAYER WHO NOW TEACHES IN INDIA AND ENGLAND. *Below* THE ANNUAL PARADE OF BRITAIN'S PONY CLUB POLO SECTION IS ALWAYS IMPRESSIVE AND THEIR CHAMPIONSHIP WEEKEND IS A FEAST OF FUN AND HARDFOUGHT GAMES.

The image of élitism works for and against polo. Obviously, there is an attraction in trying to become part of something special, but the novelty can quickly wear thin when the novice finds no clear route for progression in the sport. Some people will be lucky with the help and advice of knowledgeable friends but others will find themselves at the mercy of the unscrupulous when they try to set up with ponies, stables and all the necessary equipment. These problems are sometimes exacerbated by the disputes and disagreements between those who are already playing and should be helping the beginners. Inevitably, it is always difficult for a group of successful men with strong characters and large egos to follow the same road peacefully. Sooner or later, however, the serious beginner will have to think about joining a polo club.

Although it is a fallacy that you have to be rich to play polo, it is clearly not a pauper's game – unless the player is a professional. Yet because of the ever spiralling costs of running a successful organisation, polo clubs today have had to change with the times and allow sponsorship to help the financing of the game. Hence any assistance with funds – both for clubs and teams – is most welcome. (Television, which would attract very large sponsorship, has covered polo on very few occasions and a classic "chicken and egg" situation seems to pertain. Many cameras are needed to allow a television audience to appreciate a polo match and no company will bear risk of this cost without the guarantee of a large audience.)

Other than through the avenue of sponsorship, clubs are restrained from progress by their structure which claims to be democratic yet has, at the same time, to satisfy the varying desires and requirements of individuals, patrons and professionals. As a result, club managers, even if they want to, are not in a position to organise a programme which would, step by step, bring about improvement for all their members. Of course, there are exceptions and the exciting and brilliantly planned and run Royal County of Berkshire Club in England has come close to perfection by making a group of high-goal professionals available to all members for instruction.

Above TOP INTERNATIONAL PLAYERS, HOWARD HIPWOOD FROM ENGLAND AND MEMO GRACIDA FROM MEXICO, SHARE THEIR THOUGHTS AFTER A GAME.
Right THE CORONATION CUP IS PLAYED FOR ANNUALLY IN FRONT OF A CROWD OF MORE THAN 20,000 PEOPLE. ALWAYS AN EXCITING INTERNATIONAL MATCH, WHEN ENGLAND WINS JUBILATION IS INTENSE. A VICTORIOUS ENGLISH TEAM HOLD THE CUP ALOFT; ANDREW SEAVILL, JULIAN HIPWOOD, JOHN HORSWELL AND LORD CHARLES BERESFORD.

International polo is flourishing yet beset with many difficulties. The biggest problem is that the public wants to see the best players from each country in the teams and, with a small team of four players participating on such a large field, it is not possible for a team of varying standards to give a satisfactory exhibition. For this reason, the handicap system is a necessary part of the game and there are very few countries whose national teams have similar total handicaps.

In 1987 the Argentinians produced one answer by staging a World Cup for teams of 14 goals. Although this was a successful tournament, initially competed for on several continents and finishing in Argentina where the hosts duly won, it highlighted another problem. Pre-World War II for the famous Westchester Cup between the US and England, the ponies were shipped from continent to continent; post-war, for the Cup of the Americas between Argentina and the US, the ponies were flown. But now the enormous costs involved mean that it is only possible for this to happen once in a decade at the most. So for the World Cup finals the visitors had to play on borrowed ponies and despite the generous behaviour of the hosts, this could not substitute for their own mounts.

Annually the Hurlingham Polo Association stages the Coronation Cup at Windsor in England, which attracts a large crowd. At this event the British team has played against varied opponents. Sometimes it has been a selection of the best foreigners playing in Britain during that particular year; on other occasions the teams from New Zealand, Mexico and the United States have agreed to play. It is always an exhilarating and enjoyable event but perennially there is much discussion as to how the British team could have performed better. Except for when the incomparable Hector Barrantes – the "Royal step-father" – coached the British team, many feel that it exhibits a lack of good team co-ordination. In 1988 the leading British player did not make himself available and a possible 29 handicap team was reduced to 24 against a similar team from the United States which could have boasted 32 goals.

This throws up another area of controversy in international polo, which is: Should professionals be paid to play for their country? Many look at other sports and say "why not?" Others believe that to expect a professional to play for honour alone is a completely out-of-date concept – especially considering the risk taken by a professional playing his best ponies for his country.

Another annual international is held in the United States between the Americans and Mexico. Over the years this has taken place at varying levels of handicap, but in 1988 the two best teams available played and it was here that the Mexicans established themselves as second only to the Argentinians in the world. Since 1986, Peter Brant has staged at Greenwich, Connecticut, the classical contest between the joint forces of the US and Mexico against an Argentinian team. Argentina has won – if narrowly – and thus indisputably established its No. 1 position.

If the Greenwich results are in any doubt, a trip to Buenos Aires in November to see the Argentine Open will attest to their brilliance. Here eight teams of between 30 and 40 goals battle for what all experts will agree must be the team championship of the world. In 1987 only two foreign players participated and the incredible standard of play and ponies was hard to believe, yet established beyond doubt that Argentina leads the world at polo.

Currently in the Argentine Open there has developed a fascinating battle between the families of Pieres and Heguy. In fact it has been two brothers against three and shortly there should be four Heguy brothers in the one team. When Baptista, a fourth Heguy, joins his brothers, the intensity of the inter-family competition will further increase. In 1986 the Heguys won by one goal but in 1987 the Pieres recaptured by a one-goal margin the title which had been theirs in 1984 and 1985. With two 10-goal players to assist them – Carlos Gracida and Ernesto Trotz – the Pieres must be favourites to stay champions but speculation is rife as to the outcome in years to come.

If one travels further afield from Buenos Aires in Argentina, one sees not only where polo begins, on the *estancias*, but also an amazing speed of play at every level with hundreds of players participating in every area. Also, on many farms can be observed mares and foals together with thousands of young polo ponies of varying ages. There is a massive industry of breeding polo ponies which, apart from the thriving internal trade, are sold all over the world and over the years there has developed a brilliant expertise of polo pony training and polo horsemanship. Their speed of mental reaction transmitted by great horsemanship, often on incredible pony power, puts them head and shoulders above all others. The North Americans, by comparison, have looked slow in encounters between the two countries. This has been exaggerated by the American method of pony training, which emphasises the necessity of stopping before turning. In a recent Cup of the Americas played in Buenos Aires, all the Argentinian spectators echoed the same point: "We flowed round the field while the Americans stopped to turn."

Above 'MEMO PAPA' GRACIDA, AN IMPORTANT PLAYER IN HIS DAY, IS NOW A GREAT INFLUENCE ON HIS SONS AND THEIR COUSINS.

Right ARGENTINIAN HIGH GOAL ACTION: ALPHONSO PIERES AND HORATIO HEGUY.

With the modern international proliferation of people and ideas, the influence of the Argentinians is being felt and in the United States a change of style is taking place as a new group of young professionals rises to the top, exhibiting a classical style of striking together with increased speed around the field.

The Florida winter in America witnesses another family tussle enacted between the Pieres and the Mexican Gracida brothers, in which Memo and Carlos Gracida have been beaten into second place by the Pieres most of the time. The latter have the advantage of an enterprising, ambitious patron, the 6-goal Peter Brant, who not only plays remarkably well as anchor, but is prepared to pay whatever it takes to provide the best players and ponies. In contrast, the Gracidas have regularly changed patrons and teams and have had to produce their own string of ponies, independent of any help. Many of the Pieres victories have been achieved only in an extra chukka and the Gracidas have gained the respect and admiration of all the polo fraternity for their skill, dash and courage. Comparisons are odious when standards are so high, but it appears that the Pieres have recourse to that little extra speed of mental and physical reaction. The Gracidas stand out for the incredible way they work together and the many skilful tricks which they play with great success against everybody except the Pieres and the Heguys.

Alongside the Argentinian/Mexican contest in the Florida winter can be found the best players from the US, England and France competing in the many high-goal tournaments. These are enterprisingly staged at the beautifully designed setting of the Palm Beach Polo and Country club and at Boca Raton. The highest handicap player currently is the stylish American Owen Rinehart, who served most of his apprenticeship under the one and only Tommy Wayman and who, during the last few years, has had great success playing in England. Rapidly catching up with Rinehart are fellow countrymen Dale Smicklas – one of the world's big hitters – Californian Rob Walton, and the greatest young potential for a long time, Mike Azarro. They now clearly constitute the third best international team in the world and have the potential to progress even further up the ladder.

The English Hipwood brothers, Julian and Howard, together with Alan Kent, have been fine ambassadors for Britain in Florida. Besides winning three World Cups there, the Hipwoods have battled with great panache in hundreds of high-goal tournaments over the last decade and Alan Kent has made many friends by giving his all at every level of handicap. The three Englishmen are widely distinctive in their styles, Julian giving his best displays in the front two positions whereas Howard is far better in number 3 or 4. Julian is the quicker and no one likes to be

hurried and marked by him while Howard is a massive, consistent hitter. The brothers are instinctive athletes who once considered soccer as a career and who have gained much from their many visits to Argentina. They owe much to the British Pony Club for starting them off but one wonders just how good they might have been had they played in South America during their childhood. Since the demise of Indian polo, the British have yet to find a replacement for this training ground.

Above TIPPED FOR THE TOP, YOUNG MIKE AZZARO IS ONE OF AMERICA'S BEST AND MOST PROMISING PLAYERS.
Above left PETER BRANT HEADS UP A FORMIDABLE TEAM OF POLOISTS, AMONG THEM BEING HECTOR BARRANTES AND GONZALO PIERES WITH WHOM HE IS SEEN CHATTING HERE. ***Below left*** ALPHONSO PIERES, ONE OF TWO 10-GOAL HANDICAPPED ARGENTINIAN BROTHERS, EXAMINES HIS EQUIPMENT BEFORE A GAME.

The Macaire brothers, Lionel and Stefan, are the Hipwoods of France. Their father was the first in Europe to run a polo academy in Paris and they demonstrate the advantages of receiving good polo instruction at an early age. Lionel, now eight goals, is a brilliant hitter with the speed of a cat. He is at his best in the middle of the game at either 2 or 3 position and has played for the last decade during the winters in Florida. In 1988 his team reached the World Cup final. He has also made many appearances in England. Stefan is a seven goaler and seems to be at his best at number 4 where his big hitting is more consistent. It is strange that there is such a gap between these two brothers and the remainder of polo players in France.

Besides Florida, polo is exploding in many parts of the United States. California has the most clubs, the two most famous being the El Dorado at Palm Springs and the Santa Barbara. Both the venue for the American Open and the location of the United States Polo Association headquarters have moved several times during the past few years and now they have both come together in Kentucky. On the East Coast polo is in a very healthy state at Myopia, Mass., Greenwich, Conn., New Jersey and in the many clubs in Upstate New York. Further south in Pennsylvania, Georgia and the Carolinas, clubs are proliferating with many enthusiastic new players. At the centre of the United

States in Illinois and Ohio new recruits are pouring in. In the South, both Mississippi and Louisiana are also showing growth. Texas has an abundant inheritance of high-standard polo which is being passed on by families like the Barrys and is maintained at many clubs. Sadly, Retama, near San Antonio, with its double back-to-back grandstand and ten polo fields, is at the moment lying idle and in the hands of a bank. In many other states there are signs that polo is taking off, with hundreds of people showing an enthusiastic interest and many new clubs being founded.

Above BRITAIN'S TWO BEST PLAYERS, THE BROTHERS HOWARD AND JULIAN HIPWOOD, TALK TACTICS BEFORE AN IMPORTANT HIGH GOAL GAME.

A HAPPY GROUP ENJOYING THE EARLY DAYS OF THE SANTA BARBARA POLO
CLUB: ANDY SMITH, GLORIA HOLDEN, CECILIA AND HARRY HICKS, GLEN
HOLDEN, MARJORY WILLIAMS, JIM GUN AND JACK WILLIAMS.

It is almost unbelievable that most of the English polo clubs are now full. For the first time new clubs are needed to provide polo for the potential influx of additional players. Cowdray and Windsor are still the two leading clubs and they stage prestigious tournaments which attract sponsorship and large entries. In 1988 the British Open – despite the poor weather – was a huge success, although it was unfortunate that there was such a shortage of prepared polo grounds that often the same field was used twice on the same day when there were only two matches to be played. However, there were many excellent teams competing with players from the United States, Mexico, Chile, New Zealand, Brazil, France and Zimbabwe taking part and the two teams from the successful Royal County of Berkshire Club acquitted themselves with distinction. This club itself organises several prestigious new tournaments – adding a welcome variety to the British polo season.

Throughout Europe, there is a growing interest in the game of polo – but still surprisingly few players. Spain, Italy, France, Germany and Switzerland all have polo clubs where healthy competition, bolstered by foreign professionals, takes place but there is no sign of an equivalent increase of players as has been the experience in the United States and Britain.

THE CASTLE RUINS OF THE OLD COWDRAY CASTLE, IN THE GROUNDS OF COWDRAY PARK, PROVIDE A MAGNIFICENT AND HISTORIC BACKDROP TO THE POLO FIELDS.

LORD COWDRAY

The THIRD VISCOUNT COWDRAY has not played polo for more than 20 years, yet he remains at the centre of the game and one of its staunchest supporters. Both he and his father were chairmen of the influential Hurlingham Polo Association, the governing body of the game in England to which many other polo playing nations look for a lead. His father set out the first Cowdray Park home grounds at the beginning of this century and John Cowdray himself was one of the most influential figures in the revival of British polo after World War II.

Despite having lost an arm during that war he continued to play using a hook to hold his reins but it is as the patriarch of the Sussex club and provider of the home of the HPA that his lordship has had most influence. Under his patronage many of Britain's best young players have had their start in the game and the Pony Club polo championships enjoy Lord Cowdray's hospitality each year during August when even his personal swimming pool is made available to the young enthusiasts. It gives him great pleasure to know that one of his sons, the Honourable Charles Pearson, is an enthusiastic and skilled player.

Always one to give sound advice from the wealth of his long experience of the game, Cowdray enjoys the status of elder statesman. The team which bears his colours has an honourable history stretching from the time when Lord Cowdray himself was joined by HRH Prince Philip in the line up. That still continues and the Cowdray Park team are privileged to some first-rate coaching from the sidelines whenever their non-playing patron is present.

After more than 60 years at the centre of the game, Lord Cowdray still holds strong views that he is not afraid to put forward. He has seen many changes, not all of which he has liked, but his home is still the centre of one of the noblest country polo clubs in the world. The home of the British Open tournament and a centre of high-goal excellence, Cowdray Park remains in the forefront of British polo, thanks to the generosity and love for the sport of the first lord of the game.

LORD COWDRAY NO LONGER PLAYS POLO BUT HE REMAINS ONE OF THE GAME'S
MOST INFLUENTIAL SUPPORTERS. HERE HE ENJOYS THE POST-MATCH
CELEBRATIONS WITH KING CONSTANTINE AND GUESTS.

THE EBULLIENT MRS HELEN BOEHM, ONE OF THE GAME'S MOST
ENTHUSIASTIC PATRONS WITH S.K. JOHNSON, CHAIRMAN OF THE USPA.

POLO PEOPLE

Nothing is cheap in polo. The signs are always there – whether it is the preferred mode of transport to a game, the clothes worn or the lavishness of the post-game entertainment. Even if such obvious pointers were absent, there would be the game itself. Horses, equipment and grooms all smell of money. Even the most heavily sponsored player has money – it is the sponsorship which bestows it.

The days when polo could be characterised as a game "played by aristocrats on the other side of the field" have gone. When that witticism was coined it referred only to those of noble birth. The "aristocracy" has changed. Now one attains a degree of aristocracy with a few hundred thousand in the bank – and to that extent at least polo is still played by aristocrats.

Polo is seductive, it is difficult to say no to and people tend to play the game until they can no longer afford it. Some do give it up with age but their continued support is often most noticeable. Many a sibling is benefiting from a parent's love of polo; many a team can play because an old enthusiast is still willing to pay. Money, it might be said, is the root of all polo.

The game's most eligible bachelors, its richest patrons, best parties, latest scandals, are the stuff of soap opera melodrama and every new season brings with it a flurry of media attention. Very few newspapers and magazines treat the game as a sport – what happens on the sidelines is what makes headline news. And polo people do little to discourage this type of coverage. The days when it was deemed suitable to appear in the papers only three times in a life – at birth, marriage and death – are long since gone. The maxim for many has become "if you've got it, flaunt it".

For Helen Boehm, American head of the art porcelain empire, having her own polo team was the acquisition of a lifetime. Bearing her name, the Boehm team provided what she regarded as the ultimate luxury. It was just one more aspect of a very full, globe-trotting life that encompasses people, porcelain, palaces – and polo.

Mrs Boehm is somewhat unusual in the polo world in that she allows her enthusiasm to show. In that respect the values of the old British Raj education do tend still to prevail. Any loud behaviour is likely to come from the bars in the drinking tents rather than from the spectators' stands. Grooms, wives and girlfriends can shout, of course, but unless the match commentator asks for it, noisy support is thin on the ground. Being there, however, is often a very important factor for involvement in polo and even those on the field will admit that the social aspect can be as attractive as the excitement of playing.

Most polo is played at a low-goal level and as such does not contain the more overt social aspects of the game at its high-goal peak. The basic ingredients are always there, however, and what marks out the more popular clubs – and nowhere more so than in England – are the distinctions made between members and non-members. With a still rigidly formal system of protocol which starts with the Royal Family, there are always barriers. Security may be the excuse but it is certainly not the reason. Epitomised at the Guards Club in Windsor, this *levée* atmosphere can be experienced whenever a member of the Royal Family is playing or is in attendance.

From the central clubhouse can be found increasing rings of diminishing privilege, and wearing the correct badge can sometimes seem *the* most important factor at a Windsor (family and place) polo match. On the periphery, the public, casual visitors or those who are keen on the game but unable to afford the membership fee, are kept on the far side of the ground. Moving slightly inwards, ordinary social members have their own car park and enclosure and use of the clubhouse. On the edge of the inner ring, playing members will probably see more behind the scenes. They are more likely, too, to be helping with the organisation. They will be shown off by the day's sponsor, for without them nothing will happen. They will probably be invited to tea along with those who, for honour or payment of a higher membership fee, are nearer the epicentre.

At the very centre – in the Royal Box – will be Her Majesty the Queen or members of her family. And whether they are there or not the chief executives of the sponsoring company will certainly be found entertaining guests useful to the business.

Journalists and social commentators at such events are privilege to a rich display. However, a talk with those who like to consider themselves "real" polo people will reveal a different scene. Behind the rich façade men and women are earning their living. Grooms are working for seven days a week from dawn to dusk. Ground and office staff arrive early and go home late to ensure that things run smoothly. Players must practise constantly – often whilst earning a living during office hours – to maintain a worthy handicap. Sponsors are seeking to gain maximum exposure to justify the money spent on a day's polo. Even the wealthy patron has to ensure for himself a regular flow of cash for his team. Nothing comes easily – though in such an obviously expensive world it may seem to.

Among the spectators there is always a sturdy band of regular enthusiasts who genuinely enjoy watching this most exciting of games for its own sake. Being old hands they will know how to gain maximum enjoyment. A picnic, a glass of Pimm's, a chair, a dog – all these add to the sporting occasion. And wherever there is a club there are always local people who come along to the grounds regularly because they have discovered a love of the game.

Of course, sport – just like life – is full of anomalies and sometimes an aspect of the "increasing rings of diminishing privilege" can manifest itself in strange ways. One summer Sunday during the 1970s, at Smith's Lawn, home of the Guards Polo Club in Windsor, Nancy Reagan, wife of the United States president, arrived in state. She was in England to attend an important Royal occasion and had been invited along with many visiting dignitaries to a polo match in which the Prince of Wales was playing in a high-goal game. Her arrival was heralded by an imposing cavalcade of limousines, out of which rushed an entourage of burly secret servicemen to usher her safely into the Royal Box.

Five minutes later a single, undistinguished estate car drove up. Behind the wheel was the Queen of England, accompanied by a single personal detective. As Her Majesty parked the car the detective stepped out and came round to open the driver's door for her. The Queen had arrived at her local polo club for an afternoon's entertainment watching her son play his favourite sport.

Below PHOTOGRAPHERS ARE NEVER MORE IN EVIDENCE THAN WHEN MEMBERS OF THE ROYAL FAMILY ARE PLAYING OR WATCHING.

Left HM THE QUEEN IS ALWAYS WILLING TO ACCOMPANY THE GAME'S SPONSOR TO PRESENT PRIZES AFTER THE MATCH. **Below** TRAVELLER, WRITER AND TV PRESENTER ALAN WHICKER IS JUST ONE OF THE WELL-KNOWN FACES TO BE SEEN AMONGST THE GUESTS AT THE BIGGER POLO OCCASIONS. **Far below** NOT EVERYONE HAS TO PAY TO VIEW. MEMBERS OF THE GENERAL PUBLIC WALKING IN WINDSOR GREAT PARK ARE OFTEN SURPRISED TO BE ABLE TO SEE A GAME IN PROGRESS ON SMITH'S LAWN.

In the USA – where the British Royal Family is often mistakenly regarded as just another arm of the entertainment industry – it is the stars of film and television who are the main attraction at polo events. Larry Hagman can regularly be seen watching polo in Dallas. In Florida he has started a game, "starring" the Prince of Wales, by throwing the ball in. Thus he may not be able to play but he can participate – and the public and the media love it.

In California, where film and TV stars are thick on the ground, the Hollywood factor is much in evidence. The Sinatras may turn out to support a pet charity benefiting from a polo match or, better still, the stars themselves may actually be playing. The international nature of polo means that the travelling celebrity can usually find somewhere to play, the exclusive quality of most clubs ensuring that the recreational benefits of the sport will not be spoiled by too many ogling fans. So in California, Florida and overseas such glitterati as Alex Cord, William Devane, Doug Sheehan, Stacey Keach, Pamela Sue Martin and Stephanie Powers all play the game in an increasingly confident and skilled way. And, of course, wherever the glitterati appear, the paparazzi are sure to follow.

Celebrity involvement with polo in the US has a lengthy pedigree. In the twenties and thirties when polo was at the height of its popularity – and the game in England was still dominated by the landed gentry and the Army – in America the "old establishment" was joined by many who were

achieving new fame and fortune. As well as Presidents of the United States, presidents of large corporations – including those of the expanding film companies – were taking up polo mallets. They were joined by many of their leading men.

In the twenties, Rudolf Valentino took up the game with macho enthusiasm. In the thirties, Walt Disney bought a string of ponies, hired a teacher and recruited his employees to play. A wooden horse was brought into the studio so that they could practise their shots between breaks in filming. Director Frank Borzage and top executive Darryl F. Zanuck were bitten by the polo bug. Very soon a host of the biggest box office draws were playing the game. Spencer Tracey, Leslie Howard, David Niven, Clark Gable, Mickey Rooney, James Gleason, Tyrone Power and Will Rogers all helped attract attention to the polo field.

Above THE PALM BEACH SUN ENCOURAGES A RELAXED ATMOSPHERE AMONG SPECTATORS. *Above right* ELDORADO CLUB, CALIFORNIA; FRANK SINATRA PRESENTS THE WINNER'S CUP TO THE ALOA TEAM. *Right* RUDOLF VALENTINO, SEEN HERE IN HIS ROLE AS THE MATADOR IN '*BLOOD AND SAND*', WAS AN ENTHUSIASTIC PLAYER WHEN AT THE HEIGHT OF HIS FAME. *Far right* ACTOR AND TV STAR, BILL DEVANE, TAKES HIS TURN AT COMMENTATING ON THE GAME HE LOVES.

Above HRH PRINCE PHILIP, PATRON OF THE HURLINGHAM POLO ASSOCIATION HAS
ADMIRING WORDS FOR GONZALO PIERES, CAPTAIN OF A WINNING ARGENTINIAN CUP TEAM.
Below THE ANNUAL INTERNATIONAL POLO DAY WHEN INVITED FOREIGN TEAMS
PLAY A REPRESENTATIVE BRITISH SQUAD FOR THE CORONATION AND JUBILEE CUPS
ALWAYS ATTRACTS HUGE CROWDS OF SPECTATORS.

JORGE HERNAN VILLAMIL (***right***) IS GENERALLY RECKONED TO MAKE SOME OF THE
VERY BEST POLO MALLETS IN THE WORLD AND HE RECEIVES REGULAR ORDERS FROM THE
WORLD'S TOP PLAYERS. HERE EDUARDO HEGUY IS SEEN TRYING A STICK.

In South America, where the best polo is still played and there is a knowledgeable crowd, top players are elevated to celebrity rank by virtue of their skills on the field – rather than by their fame off it. Top-handicapped professionals such as the Harriotts, the Pieres, the Heguys and the Dorignacs receive adulation. Their names and careers are widely known, their prowess is revered and it is their gladiatorial skills which encourage large spectator crowds.

In Europe and the USA, the talents of these top South American players are known to a discerning few, and their services as professionals are hotly contested. The Argentinian Gonzalo Pieres is reputed to have secured a one million dollar contract and there is no doubt that the few most sought-after professional players can earn as much as $750,000 a year.

Professionals – not all of them South American – paid for by team patrons have become the foundation upon which high-goal and much of medium-goal polo is built. Yet although they have long existed, it is comparatively recently that they have become respectable members of the polo community. Even now very few will discuss money openly. Unofficial pay scales, based on a playing handicap, are in operation but each man negotiates his own price.

Very few teams are made up entirely of professionals. At least one of the team will be an enthusiastic amateur – the "patron" (pronounced pắt-rǒn) – and it is likely to be his money that maintains the others. Factors – besides an ability to play match-winning games – which put up a professional's price include his ability to coach a low-handicapped patron, to lead and inspire a team and to prepare and train horses.

Polo patronage is an extraordinary phenomenon. There can be no other sport in which a low-grade player can take part at the highest levels, such participation often proving both honourable and successful. It is as if an average small-town club tennis player were able to hire the services of Ivan Lendl or John McEnroe in order to win a local championship – and then compete with him in doubles at Wimbledon.

Although for most amateur players the sport is like any other which takes time, dedication, and not a little personal income, for the super-well-heeled patron polo provides just the opportunity for the rich amateur to play side by side with some of the most talented players in the world. What makes it even more astonishing is that there is little or no tangible return on the patron's investment. Prize money is virtually non-existent; the best that can be expected is usually a piece of engraved silver or glass. The pride of winning, and an exciting afternoon's sport playing with the finest in the world, is the stimulus.

As recounted in Chapter One, women have been playing polo from the beginning. The rediscovered nineteenth-century sport, however, was very much a game for men only, since society's strict mores allowed little room for well-bred ladies to step outside what was considered the norm. On the other hand, the women who helped their men govern the British Empire were on the whole a tough breed and by the turn of the century ladies once again were starting to try their hand at the game. While not encouraged to take part in the men's game, the women often formed teams of their own and enjoyed a gentle afternoon's sport. Astonishingly many female players sat side-saddle, offering what would be a somewhat bizarre spectacle for the modern eye.

It is a fact of life that – now as well as in the past – it is mainly on the sidelines that women contribute so much to the game – as paid (or unpaid) grooms, as coaches, as stick-bearers, and as encouragers and comforters. Yet this never has been – and never will be – the whole story.

By the 1920s in the USA Mrs Thomas Hitchcock Sr. not only captained her own team but was also a respected coach of many young and up-coming players – including her own son. Helen Ashton, mother of the four Australian Ashton brothers, was credited with much of her sons' success on the polo field. Indeed, when her fourth boy arrived the doctor is reputed to have said: "And now you have a polo team!"

On the contemporary scene, the most successful woman player has undoubtedly been Claire Tomlinson. From a polo-playing family now living near the English town of Cirencester in Gloucestershire, and whose father Arthur Lucas had founded a polo club in Hertfordshire, the young Claire was brought up in daily contact with the game. However, in her early years there was no question of her playing in any serious way; she took to other Pony Club equestrian activities and became proficient at most of the games she played. Even enjoying her last two years of school education at Millfield – which boasts polo as an extra-curricular activity – Tomlinson did not take up the game.

At Oxford University she won honours in both the squash and fencing teams and when the University Polo Club indicated that it was short of players it seemed natural that this extraordinary all-round sportswoman with riding skills should apply to take part. Soon she was proficient enough to take part in the annual Oxford versus Cambridge University polo match. Oxford won that year – and so did the game of polo. Claire Tomlinson was hooked.

With an honours degree in the bag, Tomlinson took her first job in Argentina, where her family had many polo-playing friends. There her standard of play improved to such an extent that on her return to England she formed Los Locos (the Mad Ones) polo team with a cavalry officer (Simon Tomlinson, whom she later married) and two other friends.

MRS THOMAS HITCHCOCK SR. WHO WAS A GREAT INFLUENCE ON MANY YOUNG PLAYERS, INCLUDING HER 10-GOAL SON. A FINE RIDER, SHE ENJOYED PLAYING AS WELL AS COACHING THE GAME.

CLAIRE TOMLINSON, THE WORLD'S HIGHEST HANDICAPPED LADY
PLAYER, WHO IS WELCOME AS A KNOWLEDGEABLE AND INTELLIGENT
PLAYER ON POLO FIELDS EVERYWHERE.

By the end of the 1960s the team had won most of the British low-goal tournaments and was beginning to take part in medium-goal games with some success. Many of the Tomlinson horses were home-bred and trained by Claire who combined the training of their string with being both a wife and mother. With good horses and plenty of practice her handicap increased to 3 goals – as did Simon's – and by 1978 they deemed their team ready to play high-goal polo. Unfortunately, the Hurlingham Polo Association had a rule forbidding women to play the game at this level, and even though Claire possessed a handicap above many of the men who were regularly enjoying top-class polo, the team was rejected.

With her friend Lavinia Black, herself a proficient player, Mrs Tomlinson organised a petition and threatened to take the Hurlingham stewards to a sex discrimination tribunal. The intransigence of the old guard quickly crumbled and the respect that she had earned ensured that the "no women in high-goal games" clause was struck from the rule book. Los Locos was allowed to play on equal terms with all-male teams and the expressed fear that women were not strong enough to compete with men was magnificently refuted when, in 1979, the Tomlinsons, joined by David Gemmell and the Argentinian Hector Crotto, won the first tournament of the high-goal season, the Queen's Cup. To prove that this was not a fluke, Los Locos went on to reach the final of the Warwickshire Cup tournament in which 14 teams took part that year. They lost by only half a goal but in the process made sure that in Britain women would forever be allowed to compete as equals.

In the Argentine, more entrenched attitudes still prevail. There is no rule preventing women from competing – but they rarely do. The macho males, when asked their opinion, tend simply to shrug. It is not that they really mind the women playing, it is just that it has never been an issue. Claire Tomlinson and other polo-playing women are not barred but they are regarded as mildly eccentric – despite the fact that in America a woman helps run one of the biggest clubs in the world, the Eldorado. As polo manager Susan Stovall finds little time to play herself but she takes delight in ensuring that the hundreds of games played each season in her east coast club proceed smoothly. She is a staunch advocate of women's polo and has been responsible for staging tournaments attracting huge numbers of women with as many as 20 all-woman teams competing.

In the USA, women's polo is a highly organised affair. Women were not given a handicap rating by the United States Polo Association until the 1970s – in Britain they have been eligible for a lot longer – and the first two to receive a rating were Sue Sally Hale and Jorie Butler Kent. Mrs Hale, who was rated in 1972, is involved in the Moorpark Polo Club in California and with her daughters, Sunset, Trails and Stormie, can now field a good low-goal team.

Right WINNERS OF THE 1987 MAYFAIR HOTEL TROPHY, PLAYED FOR ANNUALLY AT THE ROYAL COUNTY OF BERKSHIRE POLO CLUB, SUSAN STOVALL FROM AMERICA, LESLIE ANN MASTERSON FROM JAMAICA WITH THE CUP, AMERICAN ALINA CARTER AND ROWENA MURRAY FROM KENYA. *Below* SAMANTHA CHARLES AT GULFSTREAM POLO CLUB, ONE OF A GROWING NUMBER OF FEMALE PLAYERS.

Mrs Kent is a daughter of the Oak Brook club founder Paul Butler and was brought up in the game. Married to the high-goal player and patron Geoffrey Kent, she travels the world and is proving a useful coach in support of her husband's teams.

Vicky Armour was the first woman in America to play in a high-goal tournament. The sister of Red Armour, one of the world's best players, she, like Claire Tomlinson, breeds and schools polo ponies.

There have been moves in the States to apply different standards to the rating of women players, but the general consensus of opinion is that it is better that they should be able to compete on equal terms with the men. With handicaps of two and three obtained under the equality system, the case has been proved that given the training and the right horses, there need be no difference between the sexes.

The best-selling English novelist and personality Jilly Cooper, while researching her latest blockbuster based on the glamorous world of polo, came up with the theory that the higher a player's handicap, the prettier the girls with whom he surrounded himself. A glance down the pony lines and in the stands to see who is supporting whom is enough to corroborate this assessment. During her researches, she asked one of the world's top 10-goalers if he didn't constantly fall in love with the pretty wives and daughters of all the other players. "Yes," he replied, "but only for two hours at a time!"

Right JILLY COOPER (RIGHT) WITH LADY EDITH FOXWELL.
Below right ACTRESS PAMELA SUE MARTIN AT ST. MORITZ.
Far right TOP AMERICAN LADY PLAYER, VICKY ARMOUR.
Below JORIE KENT MOVES IN WITH HER CLIPBOARD AND GROOM, BRETT KIELY, TO DISCUSS THE WINDSOR PARK TEAM'S PERFORMANCE DURING THE HALF TIME INTERVAL.

With a sport so full of speed, excitement and, therefore, tension there is a great need for all those on the sidelines to support the players fully. Pre-match nerves can be as fierce for the low-goal as the high-goal player and while the game is in progress those associated with the combatants who choose to attend can expect to be treated like slaves. In the thick of a tension-filled game it is a common sight to see men and women galloping off the field waving a broken stick menacingly and screaming for a replacement – and woe betide him or her who proffers the wrong size. At least one polo girlfriend of a professional has made it a condition of her attending matches that she receives all the respect due to her – whatever the circumstances.

However, although from time to time tempers do snap and voices are raised in anger, it would be unfair to suggest that bad behaviour from players is commonplace. Indeed, most players are well aware that their on-field performance relies considerably on their back-up team and that friends and grooms have an important part to play.

The infrastructure necessary to ensure that eight mounted players, two umpires and a referee all appear on the polo ground on time in order to enjoy a game is considerable. Ground staff will have worked throughout the year to make sure that the condition of the playing field is as optimum as possible. The management team needs to understand the nature of local geographical conditions, anticipate the likely weather, purchase and maintain necessary mechanical equipment and still, on the day of play, answer criticisms levelled at it. A group of such men and women would be hard to find anywhere, yet most clubs have such staff on whom they rely completely.

The office staff also plays a vital role in any club. Organising practice chukkas and games, they are the first in line to ensure that busy executives can get the time that they want on the polo field. The ground space has to be allotted, stabling and pony line areas catered for and sometimes even the teams put together. If the club is a public one then non-playing members have to be looked after. These members can be as demanding as the players themselves, requiring seating, parking and feeding and getting most upset if arrangements do not go exactly to plan. The special needs of sponsors and their agents also need catering for. What may be a routine match within the club is probably the most important event in a sponsoring company's calendar and everything must run smoothly to ensure that guests enjoy themselves and that business for both the sponsor and the club is enhanced.

Top far left MODERN TECHNOLOGY ENSURES GOOD COMMUNICATIONS DURING A BUSY POLO DAY AT THE GUARDS CLUB WHERE HETTY DENNIS WAS SECRETARY. *Far left* EVERYTHING MUST BE IN ITS PLACE BEFORE THE MATCH AND PENNY SACKIER (LEFT) AND HER STAFF HAVE TO ENSURE THAT NOTHING GOES WRONG.

Left SORTING THE TACK CAN ALSO TAKE TIME. *Below left* EVERYONE HAS TO GIVE A HAND WHEN IT COMES TO TRANSPORTING THE HORSES. *Below right* WITH A STRING OF HORSES TO PREPARE THERE IS MUCH TACK TO BE UNLOADED.

The superb organisation of the club needs to be matched by the organisation of each individual player and his teams. The Prince of Wales' polo manager, Major Ronald Ferguson, reckons that it can be the "stable organisation" that wins a match. The *double entendre* is intentional: a player must have a stable environment based on his horses in order to function properly. Without a fit, well-cared for string of ponies a player is impotent and he must employ and manage at least one groom who will be responsible for the health of the string and for its appearing on time in the pony lines ready for each game. Together with the player he or she will have the horses listed in the correct order of play, properly tacked up and with the right spare pony in reserve.

Stable organisation must work like the smoothest of well-oiled machines – despite any difficulties. Driving the horses to various grounds can require as much organisation as any other aspect of the groom's work. Local traffic conditions must be anticipated and

mechanical transport failures quickly dealt with. It is no use to a player to find that his horses are not ready for a game. He and his team-mates rely entirely on them being there.

For many polo grooms the pay is low and the work seasonal. Yet the job requires a degree of dedication and attention to detail which is remarkable – long hours and early starts being a feature of the life. The horses are athletes that must be kept in the peak of condition. All are individuals and the differences must be recognised and incorporated into training programmes. Horseflesh itself is valuable and the animals must not be overstretched. It is not an easy job.

The player who finds good grooms is indeed lucky and it has been said that the very best can be worth an extra goal handicap. Top grooms are able to undertake all that is required, from bringing a green horse up to playing standard to ensuring the absolute readiness of the finest experienced pony for play. And a knowledge of all aspects of horse care – including some veterinary skills – is essential. An ability to understand and even play polo is also a great advantage.

It is not surprising, then, that the wisest players and patrons have always looked after their staff well. Loyalty is a strong feature of the groom-player relationship and many boast long service. Many top professional players have been grooms for others, if only members of their family. Certainly the best players are intimately involved

with all their horses and all aspects of their management and care. The great 10-goal Cecil Smith is reported to have acted as groom for his own groom, James Rice, when he played some match games in San Antonio. Prince Philip has said that the horse is no respecter of rank and nowhere is that better seen than on the polo field. Player and groom will work as a team if they want to be effective in the game. When a horse has needs, the nearest person must be prepared to do what is necessary.

Both players and grooms want their horses looking their best and healthy rivalry exists between stables. Most of the work of cleaning tack and maintaining the appearance of the mounts inevitably falls upon the groom and each takes inordinate pride in the results of their labours – as a walk along any pony line will show. There is a strong camaraderie among the workers in the lines and in individual yards (often shared by members of the same team) which speaks well of those involved. And, as with all horse sports, the veterinary practitioner and the farrier have important roles to play, keeping the ponies fit and well-shod being a shared task.

Above left ONE OF AMERICA'S BEST KNOWN GROOMS, JAMES RICE WHO WORKED FOR THE GREAT CECIL SMITH. *Below left* PRETTY GIRLS BECOME PRETTY WOMEN AND BOTH ARE WELCOME ON THE POLO FIELD. *Above* ON PLAYING DAYS THE WORK OF THE POLO GROOM CONTINUES FROM DAWN TO DUSK WITH FEW BREAKS.

OLD FRIENDS MEET AGAIN! DR VIK ADVANI AND FASHION DESIGNER
BRUCE OLDFIELD BETWEEN CHUKKAS.

Recording all that happens both on and off the field (apart from the celebrity-hungry paparazzi at main events) is a small but dedicated band of photographers and artists. Some remain attached to an individual club, while others travel from country to country following the polo seasons where they are played. In an expensive sport where the financial returns are minimal, players and patrons often spend large amounts of money on having a pictorial record of their sporting achievements on the field. Part of the attraction of the game is the thrill of man and horse being at one with a common purpose and photographs and paintings that capture this for posterity are highly prized.

Polo has more than its fair share of attractions to offer the "groupie" and wherever it is played there is found a cross-section of people who, though not players, are there

for a purpose. It may be because they have a genuine love of the sporting aspects of the game, or they may like to watch horses showing their particular qualities of courage and skill. They may be merely enjoying a day out with friends in the country, with polo the backdrop to a picnic. They may be involved in a business deal with a sponsor who is using the occasion provided by a game as a sweetener to the transaction. They may be there because they are convinced that the polo club is the place to be seen by observers of the social or fashion scene – of which they feel themselves to be an indispensable part.

Whatever the reasons for them "being there", the kaleidoscopic totality of polo people who attend helps to create the very special atmosphere that pervades this unique game.

POLO PLAYERS' PRIORITIES: WINE, WOMEN AND WINNING —
BUT IN WHICH ORDER?

MAJOR RONALD FERGUSON

MAJOR RONALD FERGUSON is the epitome of the popular idea of a polo player: descended from royal and noble lines, father of the Duchess of York, Old Etonian, former commander of the Sovereign's Escort whilst in the Life Guards and for nearly 20 years the Prince of Wales' polo manager. Handsome and dashing, the newspaper columnists call him, yet, while true, this does not really give the full picture.

Major Ferguson has served and played the game for 35 years, and as a senior administrator much of polo's modern image can be attributed directly to him. He has visited nearly every country where polo is found and is probably the sport's best-known ambassador. His groom, George Smith, has been with him for 27 seasons.

As a member of the Guards Club he instituted some of the changes which were to lead to a more professional public face for the game: punctuality, recognised uniforms for club officials such as the on-field umpires, better facilities for players and spectators alike, and many other progressive innovations. Service and standards are his watchwords and the Major has little sympathy with those who give less than their best. During his foreign travels he enjoys "fabulous hospitality – and therefore I expect to give of myself in return". One who enjoys his life immensely, Ferguson quips that "most clubs win their matches by their hospitality before the game".

As a courtier responsible for Prince Charles' polo, attention to detail has always been important to him, but ensuring the highest standards has never been allowed to get in the way of relationships. Major Ferguson is welcome wherever he goes in the tight-knit world of polo. Nowadays he admits that "the playing disease is nowhere near as bad as the administration disease but playing is still a fantastic relaxation." And it is that opportunity to relax which is offered to Prince Charles by polo that Ferguson thinks is a "fabulous public relations exercise on foreign tours. When the Prince has done his official duties, he can play six chukkas and be seen doing something manly, sporting and tough."

AS POLO MANAGER TO THE PRINCE OF WALES, MAJOR FERGUSON ENSURES
THAT HIS ROYAL HIGHNESS CAN ENJOY HIS SPORT TO THE
FULL DESPITE A BUSY SCHEDULE.

Royal involvement has helped the polo explosion which Ronald Ferguson has witnessed, and had his part in, over the past few years. So, too, has he been involved in much hard, commercial work behind the scenes and his tough negotiating ability, coupled with the giving of value for money to sponsors, have paid many dividends to the sport. Corporate involvement in the game is now taken for granted but it is men like Ferguson who have ensured that this has happened in a way that those who play the game have not felt it diminished by commercialism.

After 35 seasons of continual play Ferguson has sustained a large number of injuries, "but I don't regret it for one second. Polo is the worst disease you can possibly have . . . and I love it!"

Below AS A SENIOR UMPIRE, MAJOR FERGUSON HAS BEEN
INFLUENTIAL IN MAINTAINING STANDARDS. **Right** SUE FERGUSON
WHO IS A CONSTANT SUPPORT TO HER HUSBAND'S POLO.
Bottom A YOUNG RONALD FERGUSON WAS A MEMBER OF PRINCE
PHILIP'S WINDSOR PARK TEAM DURING THE 1960S.

CLAIRE TOMLINSON

CLAIRE TOMLINSON has a reputation to live up to. She is the highest-rated woman in polo. That can be a drawback, she says, as sometimes it marks her out from the other players and more is expected than she can sometimes deliver. One thing is certain though: she will always give selflessly as part of a team.

Passionate about her chosen sport, Tomlinson has played all over the world. In macho South America she is regarded as a mild eccentric; in the Indian sub-continent something of a celebrity; but it is in her native England that she has won the equal place that she always wanted. Coming from the polo-playing Lucas family, she began with an advantage in the game, yet polo came late in her sporting interests. After university she took a job in the Argentine where her polo rapidly improved and by the time that she formed her own team with her husband Simon, she was playing a very good game with a steadily increasing handicap. The name of her team, Los Locos (the mad ones), indicates one of her most precious resources – a sense of humour.

Tomlinson runs an important polo pony breeding establishment at her home in Gloucestershire and she often plays host to foreign, particularly South American, visitors. Others who benefit greatly from her generosity are the young. Her knowledge of the Argentinian system of instruction for young players makes here a strong advocate for encouraging skills among children (which now includes her own three). "We must get the atmosphere and environment right," she says. "Children need to ride a lot and learn to relax on a horse. I agree with the mother at one of my local Pony Clubs who said to me that polo is the only equestrian sport where a child learns to relax on a horse. It's a great sport and we should all *enjoy* it to the full."

COMPETING ON EQUAL TERMS WITH MALE PLAYERS HAS NEVER
DAUNTED CLAIRE TOMLINSON.

Although she does play all-women polo, Claire Tomlinson prefers the mixed game. "In ladies polo I'm always under a lot more pressure with two markers and so on. But polo is a team game and I should just be allowed to play my part as one of four. Mixed polo is usually of a higher standard which makes it harder but ultimately more fun."

For her it is a sport, to be played to win – but Mrs Tomlinson's contribution is more than the selfish pursuit of sporting honour. A teacher, an encourager, a scientific breeder of horses, a person with strong views who is increasingly becoming involved in the background administration of the game, she is rapidly becoming, despite her age, the matriarch of polo.

CLAIRE TOMLINSON COMBINES MANY ROLES — ONE OF THEM BEING
THE HIGHEST-RATED WOMAN IN POLO.

CLAIRE TOMLINSON'S NEPHEW WILLIAM LUCAS HAS BENEFITED FROM
HIS AUNT'S HELP AND ADVICE.

10-GOALER GONZALO PIERES IS RECKONED BY MANY TO BE THE BEST
PLAYER IN THE WORLD TODAY.

DORIGNAC AND PIERES

"IN ARGENTINA WE'RE THE BEST", boasts Francisco Dorignac, President of the Argentine Polo Association. "But that doesn't mean that we can't learn from others. We are always at school," he says, "we must always be learning." And that is what made him a 10-goal player. Even now Dorignac maintains an 8-goal handicap despite being in his fifties with a record of having played with three generations of top-class Argentinians: the Menditeguy-Alberdi-Cavanagh generation, the Harriott-Heguy dominant group; and the present Tanoira-Trotz-Pieres galaxy of superstars.

Coming from a polo-playing family (his father founded the famous Tortugas club and the young Francisco received instruction from his 10-goal handicap uncle Enrique Alberdi), Dorignac believes firmly in the need for superb organisation to back any polo-playing skills. That this thinking makes good sense is shown by the fact that he has played in the world's toughest polo tournament, the Argentine Open, since 1957, adding up to more than 30 years at the top.

"Polo in Argentina is based on the farm. Most players have a ranch or have something to do with a farm; 90 per cent of polo in Argentina comes out of this source," says Dorignac. "There we play without any limits. You start young and you play high-goal polo from the beginning. The families encourage it."

Certainly two of the current Argentine stars have been encouraged in the game by their families. Gonzalo and Alfonso Pieres both have attained the coveted 10-goal handicap and both started young. Gonzalo was playing off a 2-goal handicap by the time he was 14 and years of sacrifice to the game and taking every opportunity to learn from others has been combined with a phenomenal degree of horsemanship to make these 10-goal brothers simply the best in the world.

"We practised with our friends on the ranch. We started riding young, we wanted to become the best," says Gonzalo Pieres. "Someone told me that 60 of my relatives play polo; it's in my blood but there is a lot of pressure being at the top." A stylish and technically brilliant player, still in his early 30s, Gonzalo now spends only six months of the year in his native land. Five months in the US and one travelling provide him with an income which ensures that he can continue to ride the classiest ponies and thrill spectators wherever he plays.

THE FIELD

THE COUNTRY NEWSPAPER

WITH WHICH IS INCORPORATED "LAND AND WATER"

VOL. CLXII. NO. 4204.   SATURDAY, JULY 22, 1933   POSTAGE { INLAND, 1½D.; CANADA AND NEW FOUNDLAND, 1½D.; FOREIGN, 3D. }   REGISTERED. PRICE 1S,

TWO KEEN POLO PLAYERS FROM EAST AND WEST

King Alfonso with the Maharajah of Jaipur, after the latter's team had won the King's Coronation Cup
at Hurlingham

5

THE GAME OF KINGS

Royal and aristocratic involvement with polo is as old as the game itself, and as has been seen in Chapter One, the role-call of regal and noble enthusiasts is long and impressive. From Genghis Khan and Alexander the Great, through the Chinese T'ang emperors and Harun-al-Raschid, to the British Royal Family, wherever polo is played their passion has had a great influence on its history and development.

The connection between polo and the British Royal Family over the past 80 years began in the British colony of Malta with the setting up of a club in 1874. Soon after the club's formation one of Queen Victoria's grandsons, Prince Louis of Battenberg (later to become Admiral of the Fleet the Marquess of Milford Haven), was an active member and by the middle of the decade that followed, Prince George, then Prince of Wales and later King George V, while serving on HMS *Dreadnought*, represented the Royal Navy when they beat the Army garrison's strong team by 2 goals. The Prince appears to have had a lively time when based on the island; indeed his father, King Edward VII, paid visits to Malta in 1903 and again in 1909. On both occasions he presented cups for matches between the Army and the Navy.

Although at that time the main task of the Royal Navy was the preservation across the globe of the "Pax Britannica", their secondary role appears to have been to spread polo far and wide. Clubs were started almost anywhere that ships could land, from China to Africa, and in the West Indies where Prince George played when commanding HMS *Thrush*.

All of King George V's four sons played polo. As well as the Prince of Wales, Prince Albert (later to become King George VI on the abdication of his brother), and Prince George, Duke of Kent, were naval players, Prince Henry, Duke of Gloucester, electing for the army.

In 1910 Prince George became King on the death of his father, o it was a new Prince of Wales, Prince Edward (later King Edward VIII), who toured the Far East and India in 1922 in HMS *Renown*. Also present as part of the ship's company was Lord Louis Mountbatten, younger son of the Marquess of Milford Haven, thus second cousin to Prince Edward. Polo was played at various ports of call on the tour with Prince Edward playing as a member of the Ship's team against various local sides. It was in 1921 at Jodhpur that Mountbatten was called on to replace an absent player, not having played before. And in spite of being told unkindly by the future General Messervy that the only way to mount a polo pony was by running up from behind the animal and vaulting over the quarters into the saddle, a lifetime's passion was to take root.

Above KING ALFONSO OF SPAIN POSES FOR THE ALBUMS OF THOSE WHO
PLAYED IN THE KING OF SPAIN'S CUP IN MALTA IN THE 1930S. LORD LOUIS
MOUNTBATTEN'S TEAM BEAT THE HOLDERS, THE 2ND BATTALION OF THE
CHESHIRE REGIMENT. LORD LOUIS STANDS TO THE LEFT OF THE KING.
Right LORD LOUIS, WHO WROTE THE STILL-POPULAR *INTRODUCTION TO
POLO*, CHANGES HORSES BETWEEN CHUKKAS.

Lord Louis Mountbatten, created Earl Mountbatten of Burma in 1947, will be remembered in history as the gifted Supreme Allied Commander in South-East Asia during the closing years of World War II and as Great Britain's last Viceroy of the Indian sub-continent; to the Royal Family as "Uncle Dickie"; to the Royal Navy, in which he rose, like his father before him, to the rank of Admiral of the Fleet and commanded fierce loyalty, as "Lord Louis"; and to the Life Guards, the senior regiment in the British Army to which he was appointed as Honorary Colonel and Gold Stick-in-Waiting to the Queen, as "Colonel Dickie". In polo circles he will long be remembered as one who, though by no means a natural horseman, nevertheless dedicated himself to all aspects of the game with the same resolution that he applied to his naval career.

After his start in 1921, he played either from the South Hampshire Club near the Portsmouth naval base or the three London clubs (Roehampton, Ranelagh and Hurlingham) when in the UK. From starting with only a wooden horse on which to practise at his first home, Adsdean, when he moved to Broadlands one of his first

tasks was to have a practice pitch constructed.

In 1926 Mountbatten arrived in Malta with, as his friend and brother-officer Andrew Yates remembers, "A three-goal handicap and lots of enthusiasm". Enthusiasm there certainly was, for over the next 12 years he was solely, or in the case of International Rules, partially responsible for establishing three landmarks in the history of the game. The first was the invention of the Royal Navy Polo Association (RNPA) head for a polo stick. Although, when the game came to the West in the previous century, the first design of heads had been with flattened sides, the only subsequent development thereafter had been the adoption of the cigar-shaped, or Jodhpur, head. By in effect squashing the existing design, much as one might tilt the face of a golf club, a player could ensure that he could loft the ball over the heads of the other players. Although not of tremendous value to forward players, who need maximum length rather than loft from their shots, it was of great use to those playing at positions number 3 or Back, both of whom for much of the time want to ensure that their shots do not get deflected by other players.

Mountbatten's second milestone was the production in 1931 of his book *An Introduction to Polo* by "Marco", his pseudonym. In his Preface to the first edition, the late Earl of Kimberley, who gained his fame as an international polo player, wrote: "On reading the book I was interested to find that it contained perhaps the most reasoned and progressive introduction to the game . . . that I have ever read. No attempt was made to investigate the theory of horsemanship, but the beginner could learn enough of the aids and their application to control a pony on the polo ground." It was an ideal no-nonsense book for the young officer about to join a polo-playing station or garrison. The book also contained superimposed instructional photographs showing the "before and after" of particular strokes, in themselves an achievement to produce in the 1930s.

Mountbatten's final legacy took place in 1938 when, as Chairman of the Hurlingham Rules Committee, he met the Chairman of the United States Polo Association and formed an International Rules Committee. This was thought to be necessary as many countries were beginning to interpret the rules, as originally laid down by Hurlingham, in differing ways. Although the USPA never accepted the final outcome, their rules only differ marginally from those of the HPA, which was to absorb those made by Mountbatten's committee.

World War II brought polo, in Europe at least, to an abrupt halt. Before Mountbatten was moved on to higher command, he saw action in the Mediterranean, losing his ship HMS *Kelly*, together with over half of the ship's company. Serving also in the Royal Navy at that time was his young nephew, Prince Philip of Greece. A combination of postwar austerity coupled with a radical socialist government was hardly conducive for the re-starting of polo in England. By 1947, however, play was in progress again, notably at Cowdray Park, and abroad the Army and Royal Navy did what they could to pick up the reins once more. Mountbatten, once his Viceregal duties were over, returned to sea, in particular to the Mediterranean, and before long Prince Philip, by now married to King George VI's heir presumptive, Princess Elizabeth, was receiving polo tuition from him in Malta.

Above LORD LOUIS MOUNTBATTEN PRESENTS THE CORONATION CUP TO
EDDIE MOORE (LEFT) AND ANTONIO HERRERA OF ARGENTINA. HE
RETAINED HIS INTEREST IN THE GAME RIGHT UP TO THE TIME OF HIS
DEATH AND HIS ADVICE TO PLAYERS WAS ALWAYS WELCOMED.
Left PRINCE PHILIP, LIKE HIS SON, TOOK EVERY OPPORTUNITY TO PLAY
POLO ON HIS FOREIGN TRAVELS.

HRH PRINCE PHILIP TAKES PART IN A COSTUMED CELEBRATION OF THE
HISTORY OF THE GAME.

Following the death of her father, Elizabeth II was crowned Queen in 1953. Prince Philip, now a Commander, left the Service (and Malta) and played for three seasons at Cowdray Park before founding the Guards Polo Club in the Great Park which contains the Royal seat of Windsor Castle. Mountbatten, by then well into his fifties, gave up active participation in the game at around this time, though continuing to give support to Prince Philip, and later to Prince Charles. In particular his stud groom, Arthur Birch, trained many of the early Royal ponies. In later years the Queen herself was to take a great interest in the breeding of polo ponies, and at one stage in the 1980s, Prince Charles was entirely mounted on "home-bred" ponies which were trained for him by his own head groom, Argentine-born Raul Correa.

In 1971, at the age of 50 and having reached a 5-goal handicap, Prince Philip finally gave up polo. His participation had undoubtedly helped to popularise the game, both with spectators and with those who were in a position to take up the sport, given an incentive. Also, as a totally uncalculated spin-off, polo at Windsor has given the Queen's subjects a unique opportunity to see her and the Royal Family close-to and other than on the TV screen. Although the Queen and Prince Philip attend less frequently now than before, today it is the turn of the following generation. Prince Charles plays whenever his duties allow, and he is often accompanied by the Princess of Wales and sometimes by their two sons, Princes William and Harry. Another Royal spectator is the Duchess of York who, before her marriage to Prince Andrew in 1986, as plain Sarah Ferguson used to walk to the grounds from her school nearby to watch her father, Major Ronald Ferguson, play. (Princess Anne, the Princess Royal, confesses to having swung a stick on a pony as a teenager, but no more, while Princes Andrew and Edward show no interest.)

Prince Charles himself was 15 when he started to take more than a passive interest in polo. His early attempts were private affairs – instruction on a wooden horse and stick-and-ball sessions on the lawns of Windsor Castle during the school holidays. In 1964 he started to play in matches at the nearby Guards Polo Club and at the end of his first season had his rating raised to −1 goal. His first success in tournament polo came when, as an 18-year-old, the Windsor Park team (Prince Charles, Prince Philip, Colonel Gerard Leigh and Captain William Loyd) beat Ronald Ferguson's Dummer team in the final of the Combermere Cup.

By the middle of the 1970s Prince Charles's handicap had risen steadily to 3 goals. Perhaps the rise would have been faster had he been able to devote more time to polo; as it was the game took very much second place to spells at Cambridge University (where he was awarded a Half Blue for representing the University at polo) and in both the Royal Navy and the Royal Air Force. The year 1973 saw his first venture into 22-goal polo when he played with Mark Vestey's Foxcote team. Naval duties kept the Prince away from high-goal polo until 1977. In that year he played with the Argentine Luis Sosa Basualdo, at that time married to Lord Cowdray's daughter Lucy, and also had his first taste of international polo, playing for Young England against France (France won by one goal). The following year saw his rise in handicap to 4 goals and his becoming a member of Guy Wildenstein's Diables Bleus. Since 1987 he has played high-goal polo with Geoffrey Kent for Windsor Park, while for seven years he has played for Galen Weston's Maple Leafs at medium (18 goal) level.

A BEARDED PRINCE CHARLES, HOME FROM HIS NAVAL DUTIES AT SEA, WAS RELIEVED TO PLAY HIS BELOVED SPORT AGAIN.

Playing with professional players whose ability easily outstrips one's own means different things to different people. Major William Loyd, who was for ten years Polo Manager at Windsor, feels that, at heart, the Prince probably prefers medium goal. That is not because the standard is lower – indeed there is no room for a passenger in the cut and thrust of English medium-goal tournaments, but rather that he wishes to be closely involved in whatever he does and above all to make a positive contribution to a team effort. This is easier to achieve playing at number 2 position with Maple Leafs than it is at Back with Windsor Park. Although he is what the English like to call a "good loser", there is little doubt that he prefers to win.

Prince Charles has suffered the loss of two relations with polo connections. The first was the death in an accident of his cousin Prince William of Gloucester in 1972. As the elder son of the Duke of Gloucester, Prince William would in due course have inherited the title. He, too, was a

member of the Guards Polo Club at Windsor, and with a handicap of 1 goal and great enthusiasm, he could have become a most respectable member of any team. The other loss was the murder of Mountbatten by terrorists while he was on holiday in the Irish Republic during the summer of 1979. "Uncle Dickie" had not only been largely responsible for the marriage of Prince Charles's parents in 1947, but had also been a mentor to the Prince from adolescence onwards – and as such he was sorely missed. In the following year Prince Charles presented a cup, the Mountbatten Cup, to the Guards Polo Club in his memory. It is played for annually by medium-goal teams from across the country during the club's Ascot Week tournaments.

Above PRINCE CHARLES JOINED HIS FATHER IN PLAYING DURING THE 1960S. THE QUEEN IS ALWAYS PLEASED TO PRESENT PRIZES TO MEMBERS OF HER FAMILY.

Another of Lord Mountbatten's great-nephews started to play polo in 1984. George, 4th Marquess of Milford Haven, had originally intended to play at Windsor with his cousin, but elected in the end to join Cowdray Park Polo Club. An enterprising businessman, George Milford Haven (for he is George to everyone) is the epitome of the popular idea of a polo player. Aristocratic, rich and dashing enough to get into the gossip columns, he pilots his own helicopter from his country seat in Essex or his smart London flat to the polo fields of Europe. In only a few years of involvement in the game he has entered at its highest level, playing always to win but with an enjoyment of the sport that is a great encouragement to all. With, next to the Prince of Wales, probably the finest polo pedigree in the world, Milford Haven has brought to the game an élan which has shocked many of the "old guard".

By dint of hard work and ingenious marketing skills, both of the teams that he runs, at medium- and high-goal level, are heavily sponsored. The commercial nature of this enterprise surprised many but has been welcomed in Britain as an advancement for many young players. Other teams are individually sponsored but they rely on the fact that a senior member of the sponsoring body is playing in the squad. Milford Haven is making outside sponsorship work for him and the two separate deals entirely pay for his polo. This is just as well since he readily admits that his intense enjoyment of and involvement in the game sometimes does get in the way of his business life.

Above LADY CRIGHTON BROWN PRESENTING A CUP TO TOP PLAYER AND TEACHER PETER GRACE.

Above GEORGE MILFORD HAVEN ARRIVES BY HELICOPTER. A KEEN
FLYER, HE HAS HIS OWN MACHINE WITH ITS CALL SIGN G-ORGE.
Right THE MARQUESS OF MILFORD HAVEN WHO HAS PERHAPS THE
FINEST POLO PEDIGREE IN THE WORLD HAS TAKEN ENTHUSIASTICALLY
TO THE SPORT.

Aware of his value, His Royal Highness The Prince of Wales allows his involvement in the game to make money in a discreet way for the numerous charities in which he takes an interest. Almost whenever he plays sponsors of that day's match are encouraged to make a donation to a named charity over and above their sponsorship fee. No extra promises are made but the likelihood of the Prince finding time for a cup of tea with the sponsor and his guests after the game are probably increased by such charitable generosity. Prince Charles, as heir to the throne, has a necessarily restricted life, but it is typical that he uses even the time he takes for rrcreational activity to good ends.

His cousin the Marquess of Milford Haven is far less restricted in his lifestyle and when his sponsors pay for a day of polo he is more than likely to be found putting out programmes on the guests' seats before they arrive. Complete involvement is important, he feels, and after a light lunch with his sponsor's clients in the marquee he excuses himself in order to change for the game. Even if afterwards he can depart for home in his personalised helicopter with its G-ORGE call-sign he is the last to leave and then only when he is satisfied that everyone has had the necessary good time and is happy that his sponsors are completely satisfied with the day.

Titles certainly help in the setting of the scene which makes modern polo a marketable commodity. The chance to meet a Prince of the Royal blood or member of the House of Lords still acts as a powerful magnet in most parts of the world. Even republican France advertises that the Marquess of Milford Haven is taking part in the Gold Cup competition in Deauville – in a list of names that omits four of the six current 10-goalers in the world. That a 3-goal handicapped player gains this accolade speaks for itself but in no way denegrates Milford Haven's involvement.

When Prince Charles is due to play anywhere, then things often become positively frantic. Fortunes are offered and many friendships made and broken as local socialites fight for the chance to appear alongside the Prince or at least be able to say "I was there". Such popular appeal does polo no harm, increases the game's charisma, and is bravely accepted by those affected. Thus Mountbatten's heirs continue to do their bit for the advancement of the sport.

Few polo players are seen today from India, the cradle of polo. Many were the maharajahs who played in the UK before World War II, but, after the war and after the partitioning and the granting of Independence to the sub-continent – for which Mountbatten was in part instrumental – few returned to play again.

Chief amongst those who did was Rao Rajah Hanut Singh. Hanut, as he was known, was the youngest son of the sometime Regent of Jodhpur, and as such was sent to war at the age of 14 with the Jodhpur Lancers in France. After the Great War he was able to concentrate on polo, captaining the Jaipur team from 1931–38. Playing as the Jaipur Tigers, a team which included "Jai", the previous Maharaja of Jaipur, they came to England in 1933 and won the Hurlingham Champion Cup.

Hanut, who at his peak was rated at 9 goals, came back to Cowdray Park to continue playing until he was 72 years old. His final triumph, when handicapped at a modest 4 goals and in his sixties, was to win the Cowdray Park Gold Cup for Eric Moller's Jersey Lilies in 1964, and again in 1965. The team was the lowest handicapped in the Open tournament on both occasions, the other team members being the young Argentinians Eduardo Moore and Ricardo Diaz, and the young Rhodesian Patrick Kemple,

who was later to be killed in his country's guerrilla war. Hanut, who always had words of encouragement for young players, is remembered as a wonderful team captain as well as being a superb horseman.

"Jai" also returned to base himself at the then fledgling Guards Polo Club at Windsor for the summers. He continued playing until his sudden death at the Cirencester Park Polo Club in 1970. His widow, the present Rajmata, was an outstanding beauty in her day and had been deeply committed to politics in Rajasthan after Independence. She still watches polo at Windsor and all over the world, always immaculate in a sari, especially when teams play once a year for the Jaipur Trophy, a gold-plated model of a horse. Jai's son, the present Maharaja, has played a few times in the UK, but not on a regular basis. He is President of the Rajasthan Polo Club in Jaipur, where he spends most of his time.

Colonel Maharaj Prem Singh, "Prem" to his friends, was another pre-war player to return to the UK. He was still playing tournament polo in the early 1970s, but now, still very active, confines himself to holding polo clinics for young players at the clubs at Cirencester and Kirtlington Park.

Polo in both India and Pakistan is now largely the

prerogative of their respective armies. India sends over a team at medium-goal strength for the occasional lightning tour of the UK (of necessity on borrowed ponies) and in return acts as most generous host to invited British teams. Although individual Pakistanis play when "passing through", contacts are now few.

Left SUCH WAS THE IMMENSE WEALTH OF POLOISTS IN THE 'GOLDEN AGE' THAT SCENES LIKE THIS WERE NOT THAT UNUSUAL. HERE THE NAWAB OF BHOPAL'S STRING OF HORSES ARE BEING EXERCISED BY THEIR INDIVIDUAL NATIVE GROOMS AT WESTONBIRT IN GLOUCESTERSHIRE, GETTING ACCLIMATISED FOR THEIR COMING GAMES AGAINST ENGLAND.
Above right THE MAHARAJA OF JAIPUR RECEIVES THE CORONATION CUP FROM THE KING AND QUEEN AT RANELAGH. JAIPUR WAS FANATICAL ABOUT HIS POLO AND REGULARLY BROUGHT HIS WINNING TEAM TO BRITAIN. **Right** MAHARAJ PREM SINGH FROM JODHPUR WHO WAS ONE OF INDIA'S TOP PLAYERS.

THE EARL AND COUNTESS OF BATHURST AT THEIR CIRENCESTER PARK
POLO CLUB WITH PONIES BROUGHT FROM THE ARGENTINE BY JACK
WILLIAMS (RIGHT) AND THEIR GROOM JUAN MURIEL.

The hereditary rulers of former British colonies in the Far East were left with a few more trappings of their former glory than were the previous rulers of the Indian States. Brunei, which still has a special relationship with Great Britain, found oil comparatively recently and the Sultan decided to spend part of his enormous revenues in creating from scratch a polo complex in what had been jungle. The result, within the limitations of humidity and heat that bedevil any such enterprise in the tropics, is a success. The Sultan of Johore, on the other hand, had always enjoyed his polo. His state was occupied by the Japanese during World War II. However, once the war was over, a large British presence was still needed to combat the communist insurgency which started soon afterwards. Thus many a young officer started his polo in Johore, where the Sultan was a most generous host. Many a tale, some apocryphal, survives from the fifties to this day; guests would sometimes be mounted on runaway ponies which would carry their riders at speed far into the jungle; and there was the time that a tiger carried off the goal-judge.

In the late 1970s, the Sultan of Pahang decided to play in England with his two sons, Tunku (Prince) Mahkota and Tunku Abdul Rahman. Lord Patrick Beresford arranged all the details for him, and in 1979 Pahang won both the Royal Windsor Cup (medium-goal) and the Archie David Cup (low-goal) on the same day. Disaster of a sort then struck, as Eddie Pahang was suddenly made King (Yang di-Pertuan Agong) of Malaysia (the State Rulers take it in turn) and the Constitution stated that the King must not leave his native shores during his time in office. Accordingly the family departed for home.

The Sultan of Oman, also newly oil-rich, does not play himself, but encourages and finances a national team. They came to England in 1985, captained by the New Zealand professional Paul Clarkin, the high point of their visit being a win over a team of similar handicap captained by Prince Charles, who was also beaten in that year by a team captained by Crown Prince Hassan bin Talal of Jordan. The Crown Prince, a jovial character who plays most of his polo with Jordanian army officers in Amman, gave Prince Charles a personal gift of some value after the game was over. Idly, Prince Charles asked him what he would have been given had the Crown Prince's team lost. This was clearly considered as a tremendous joke, and when his laughter subsided the Crown Prince replied, "Why, nothing!"

Although polo has been established for far too short a time in the Western world for there to be any talk of polo dynasties, three families – those of Cowdray, Bathurst and Beresford – come closest to this description. The Cowdray Park Polo Club was started by the 2nd Viscount Cowdray on his family estate in Sussex in 1910. His son, Lord (John) Cowdray, inherited just before World War II, but soon afterwards lost his left arm whilst fighting with the British Expeditionary Force in Europe. To many, this would have signified an end to polo, but not to Cowdray. Not only did he continue to play after the war until into his late fifties, but also it was he who was largely instrumental in reviving interest in polo in the UK as a whole. With an eye to the future, he ran a large string of ponies which he would arrange to be hired out on a chukka basis at a very cheap rate, there being no charge at all for army officer cadets.

Although Cowdray has accepted sponsorship in recent years for the British Open Championship, he does not openly seek it. To sit in the sun on his lawn grounds on a summer's afternoon with the ruins of Cowdray Castle as a backdrop and a glass of Pimm's in one's hand is one of the most pleasant ways to pass the time. Although Lord Cowdray no longer plays, he still runs a Cowdray Park team, captained by the latest in line, his younger son Charles.

The present Earl Bathurst's grandfather, the 7th Earl, founded the Cirencester Park Club on his estate in Gloucestershire. The famous Ivy Lodge ground was put to the plough during the war, consequently it was not until 1952 that Lord Bathurst and his brother George restarted the club. Lord Vestey and his brother Mark were great supporters of the club until the start of the 1980s, their teams Stowell Park and Foxcote regularly winning the major trophies from the other clubs.

Although the Republic of Ireland is not part of the United Kingdom, paradoxically it is so regarded for polo purposes. Thus the protectionist rules that the Hurlingham Polo Association lays down from time to time which restrict the number of "foreigners" that may play in one team do not apply to the Irish. Indeed, the All Ireland Polo Club, based at Phoenix Park, three miles from the centre of Dublin, is firmly affiliated to Hurlingham.

Phoenix Park is also the home club for the 8th Marquess of Waterford, head of the Beresford family. The Beresfords have a long and distinguished tradition of service to the British Crown, either as soldiers or sailors, and both the Marquess and his younger brother served with the Royal Horse Guards. Lord Patrick was a regular officer, and was later to serve with the Guards Parachute Company and

with the élite SAS. Both brothers achieved 4-goal ratings when playing at Windsor and, although Lord Waterford tended to be a summer visitor, having his estates to care for in County Waterford, Lord Patrick put down his roots in Berkshire.

The Marquess is currently playing off 2 goals, but nevertheless could provide a 15-goal side from within his own family without needing to incorporate his brother. His son and heir, Henry, Earl of Tyrone, currently plays at Cirencester off a 4-goal handicap. Lord Charles Beresford (7 goals) is an international player who represented England in their victory over North America in 1988; and Lord James, the youngest, plays off a modest 2 goals at Phoenix Park. If reserves were to be needed, in addition to his brother, his cousin Major Hugh Dawnay lives in the same county, where he runs his own polo club, Whitfield Court, and plays off 3 goals.

LORD CHARLES BERESFORD; JUST ONE OF THE LARGE POLO PLAYING FAMILY FROM IRELAND.

THE SKILLS OF THE RIDER ARE NEVER MORE TESTED THAN WHEN ON THE POLO
FIELD. HORSES MUST RESPOND TO EVERY COMMAND FEARLESSLY AND QUICKLY.
DEVELOPING THE NECESSARY TRUST TAKES TIME AND GREAT PATIENCE.

THE GAME OF KINGS AND THE KING OF GAMES; POLO OFFERS ITS
EXCITEMENTS TO ALL CLASSES.

QUITE SIMPLY, THE HORSE IS THE SUPREME BEING OF THE GAME. THE
BEST PLAYING PONIES HAVE ALWAYS COMMANDED HIGH PRICES.

6

THE KINGS OF THE GAME

Alan Kent, a top English player, is remembered at his old school Millfield (where polo is one of the extra-curricular activities offered) as the boy who defied matron to sleep with his pony when it was ill. That devotion to his horses has continued and he is convinced that it is the key to his success as a polo player. Nor is he alone in this devotion. Argentinian Gonzalo Pieres reckons that in order to maintain a high handicap the strength of a player's string of ponies must also be maintained. His brother Alphonso, also a 10-goaler, emphasises that he plays polo because of his love of horses. New Zealander Stewart Mackenzie suggests that the variations in a player's ability at the upper levels can often depend on the quality of his horses.

It has been pointed out by Julian Hipwood, long-time captain of England's national side, that you cannot hit the ball if you do not get to it – and it is the horse that achieves this. Going flat out a galloping horse reaches speeds of up to 40 mph (65 km/h). Much is asked of it; it will have to stop suddenly, turn quickly and be prepared to ride into another horse to push it and its rider off the line of the ball.

It is received wisdom in polo circles that the horse constitutes at least 75 per cent of the game. Offered with conviction whenever it is uttered, this theory is open to scrutiny. If all other factors between two teams were equal – playing ability, umpiring, ground conditions and so on – but the two strings of ponies were unevenly matched, then undoubtedly the team with the best horses would win the game. In such a case the horse could be said to be the 100 per cent deciding factor. However, such a state of affairs can never exist. Individual players are different in their ability, even from one day to the next; umpiring can be uneven; a whole host of conditions on a playing field might well favour one team over another.

A poor team, or one having a run of poor co-ordination, will not beat a better team playing precise and good team polo even if they are mounted on more brilliant horses. Of course, if the better team are so poorly mounted that they lose the match, then again the horse might be said to have constituted 100 per cent of the outcome. But it is too easy to offer a percentage figure which intends to give credit to the horse but probably is more likely to allow the hearer to nod wisely and miss the point.

A good horse cannot really make up for a player's deficiencies – but it can make a competent player a better one. The same horse will not necessarily work well for different people and it is not possible to play a better game than the horse will allow. One thing is certain: polo cannot be played without the horse and therefore the search for better animals is constant at all levels of the game.

All players dream of having a good string from which to choose ponies for each day's game. And to make his dreams come true a patron with little time to spend with his horses will sensibly employ a professional especially proficient in this field. In the golden age of the game in India it was not unknown for a maharaja to maintain a string of 60 ponies, each one with its own groom to care for it. Those days are long gone but some of the top players and patrons still maintain big barns full of the best horseflesh. They know that such is the way to win in polo.

A high-goal team will need at least 26 horses on which to call, though all of them will not necessarily be played every game. Polo is a tough sport and the animals – like the players – do not always remain sound so some have to be kept in reserve. The low- and medium-goal player can operate on only a few horses, yet as much concern in the buying and care of them is required.

What makes a good polo pony is a matter of debate and certainly there is no single answer. Breeding is a complex business and the end result might please one person and not another. The best ponies are found out in play. They may not look very beautiful, but if they play the game well then that is all that is required.

Over the years no breed has established itself as *the* polo pony. Crossbreeds have excelled in the game and as such have come to be fully accepted. Thus polo ponies are a type, not a breed. They have no stud book and no authenticated pedigrees. Types are produced by cross-breeding and no breeding is absolutely true to type. Playing ability is all that counts in the final analysis.

From the middle of the seventeenth century the English Thoroughbred horse was developed over a period of 200 years into the fastest and most valuable breed in the world. Few speed records have been broken in the last 100 years and the Thoroughbred is highly regarded as an animal which can be used to "upgrade" other breeds. If not Thoroughbred, most present-day polo ponies have a very high proportion of Thoroughbred blood flowing through their veins.

There has been a dramatic change in the use of the horse in the past century. From being an essential work animal it has become mostly a creature of leisure and sport. This has vastly changed the breeding of mounts, which has evolved into a multi-million-dollar industry with the serious money changing hands in racing and showjumping. Polo has benefited from this change and many old breeds have

been given fresh blood to make them more suitable for the game.

Sports horses fall into two categories: hot-blooded and warm-blooded. These refer to a difference in pedigree and character rather than the body temperature of the animal. The hot-blooded beast is of the purest blood, an Arab or a Thoroughbred, and has great spirit. The warm-blooded horse is a mixture and will usually have as its progenitor a hot-blooded breed. The mixture might even include some cold-blood (from the German *Kaltblütigkeit*, meaning calmness and solidity – the attributes of the slower, heavier workhorse). The warm-blood is not as high spirited as the hot-blood or as slow as the cold-blood. It is bred for a purpose and on the whole has a character which is trainable.

The warm-blooded horse is thus most likely to be found in a polo stable. Many trainers and players like to take horses from the race track and some brilliant polo ponies are Thoroughbreds from this source, but the majority tend to be mixtures.

Although, once they had mastered the rudiments of play, British Army officers soon began to use the horses which were most easily obtainable, the first modern polo mounts were true ponies of about 12 hands high from India. These Manipur ponies, thickset, quick and manoeuvrable animals, descended from the Asiatic Wild Horse and the Arab, proved useful for the game. In the nineteenth century most remounts came from Australia and were known as "Walers" because they were first bred in New South Wales. These hardy, versatile ponies quickly adapted to the game and were generally much favoured. A cross between Arab, Thoroughbred and Anglo-Arab stallions which were put with local mares and cobs, the Waler has since been rechristened the Australian Stock Horse. Tough and agile, the Waler was much favoured by the great British-Indian player, writer and teacher Sir Beauvoir de Lisle.

Left MANY OF THE CURRENT STOCK OF POLO PONIES HAVE BEEN BRED FROM THOROUGHBREDS FROM THE RACECOURSE. *Above* EXPERTS ENDLESSLY DISCUSS WHAT MAKES FOR A GOOD POLO PONY, BUT WHEN ONE IS FOUND THEN EVERYONE KNOWS.

In the 1890s, attempts to produce a top-rate polo pony were begun in Great Britain when Thoroughbreds were crossed with some of the native Mountain and Moorland pony breeds. The outbreak of World War I disrupted this programme and by the time polo had been restarted the height limit had been abolished. By the early 1920s players could ride any animal which suited them and this effectively ruled out the need for such specific experiments.

In America the Quarter Horse, a nimble and sensible animal used on the ranch for stock work, came to be favoured as a polo mount. So-called because it was raced over a quarter of a mile race track to test its considerable speed, the Quarter Horse was a favourite with the cowboy because of its balance and easy ability to stop and start – qualities which well suited it to polo. The Argentinian cowboy, the *gaucho*, was riding a similar horse descended from a group of Andalusian horses brought to the New World by the Spanish which had escaped to roam wild. The Criollo is a tough, manoeuvrable and enduring horse ideally suited to ranch work. Crossed with the Thoroughbred it, too, produced an ideal polo pony.

Today the vast majority of polo ponies come from the Argentine. Some 2,000 animals are exported each year and Francisco Dorignac, President of the Argentine Polo Association, reckons that his country has a movement of 40,000 polo ponies during any one year. Half of these are being played regularly and half are "green" horses being brought on into the game. Local horses are used in all parts of the world where polo is played but the sheer weight of Argentinian numbers and brilliance of their trainers and players ensure that the South American pony reigns supreme.

MOST AGREE THAT THE BEST PONIES ARE BRED IN THE ARGENTINE.
HERE A CLUSTER OF PREGNANT MARES CROSSES A WATERING PLACE IN
THE ESTANCIA EL BONETE.

As has been pointed out, a polo pony is judged solely by its performance on the field, and Billy Wayman, the father of the 10-goaler Tommy and an accomplished horse trainer, is convinced that a polo pony is born not made. Others may disagree, but few would quarrel with the view that the polo pony is unique in the equine world, being trained to answer to the rider's commands in the heat of competition to an extraordinary extent.

The requirements of a polo pony fall into a number of broad categories. Most are now between 15 and 16 hands, bought according to the size preference of the rider. At the number 1 and Back position in the team the horses generally are thought to require most speed. In the central number 2 and 3 positions a boldness and handiness is more often required.

Grooms may be the first to suggest that above all the horse must show an ability not to play up or misbehave in the pony lines. Travelling and being with others will be a feature of its life and if it is upset by this it will be of little use. (According to many a stable worker, a pleasant disposition and good attitude to the game are requirements of both horse *and* rider.) It must be fast and able to gallop and accelerate when asked to do so. Ability to start in a straight line, stop and turn quickly are essential. The horse must be tough, courageous, spirited, agile, bold, versatile, enthusiastic; it must be strong and able to rate itself; it must have a robust conformation and be healthy . . . the things to be desired are endless, it seems.

A look along a pony line will reveal animals of many shapes and sizes. All will look like athletes, with angular bodies, very strong backs and quarters and correct, sound limbs with well-formed feet. Most will have been carefully trained to perform to the limits of their playing ability. Many will have been bred especially, some will have been chosen from another discipline to perform their task. Everyone is looking for a horse that is easy to play, if not to ride. As riding constitutes perhaps 95 per cent of the game and hitting the ball only 5 per cent, a comfortable ride is also much sought after. Every horse will certainly be highly prized by its owners – whatever the price that was paid for it.

A pony must not play more than one chukka without a break and it is most unlikely to play more than two periods in a game. Until the start of the chukka in which each one will be used, the successful polo player thinks more about his horses than himself. But from that moment the player will cease to think of his mount – just so long as it is going well and has nothing obviously wrong with it. For about seven minutes the pony is merely a machine that must play

its part in the game, causing no upset and doing exactly what is asked of it. This may seem a hard attitude – but there is no alternative. As part of a team with major responsibilities, the rider has many other things to think about.

Polo is a tough sport and the horses – like the riders – will inevitably experience knocks, discomfort and sometimes pain, but this is minimised as much as possible with protective bandages on the legs and rules which prize safe play above all else. Of course, the sensitive rider will be aware of any problems with his horse and the rules require that the game stops immediately if a horse or its tack needs attention. Mounts are not just valuable in money terms, they represent a great investment by the owner in time and attention and most players enjoy a relationship with their horses which quickly allows them to spot trouble and deal with it kindly.

Above left TREATED AS A MACHINE WHILST PLAYING, THE HORSE IS NONE-THE-LESS LOVED BY ITS OWNER OFF THE FIELD. *Above right* PRINCE CHARLES GIVES A SUGAR LUMP TREAT AFTER THE GAME. *Right below* ACCIDENTS DO HAPPEN BUT THE GAME STOPS IMMEDIATELY AND HORSES AND RIDERS ARE USUALLY NONE THE WORSE FOR THEIR FALLS.

Every aspect of correct breeding and training – the business of bringing an animal to the polo field – is both complex and critical and varies from place to place and trainer to trainer. The amount of land and stock available will often determine the price of a horse and the time taken over its training. A sensitive choice of parents – ensuring that they are both of sound stock – will be made, the virtues of the stallion being used to correct the faults of the mare. When resources are in short supply, as in Europe, a breeder will have to make the best of whatever he or she produces. In South America a horse that does not turn out well will simply be returned to the ranch. Either way, "getting the blood right" is an important first consideration, with most breeders wanting to keep at least some basic Argentine Criollo blood in the animal, adding Thoroughbred and constantly looking also to add the particular special qualities from other breeds.

Early training will vary little from that of other sporting horses. They will be brought on slowly and worked with their future career in mind. The best ponies are not broken too young and are allowed to "put on the miles" gently in open spaces. Reckoned to be at its playing peak between nine and twelve, a good pony can go on until it is twenty, with time taken at the beginning of the training process added in multiples to the end of a horse's working life. The advantages of being able to work a horse with the stock on a ranch, as in the Americas and Australasia, are immense. Here, a young, green animal becomes fit and agile, will learn to stop, turn and start nimbly; and will gain a great sense of balance. Work of this nature from the age of three or four for a couple of years can be the making of a successful polo pony.

A pony will not usually be brought to the game of polo much before it is four or five years old. At this point the importance of the horse's early experiences will be noted. Most horses possess much native instinct, which can be either used or marred; few are entirely bad but many can be turned so by faulty handling or inconsiderate training or riding. As Billy Wayman notes: "A horse can remember – but he can't think."

Patience is undoubtedly the greatest quality possessed by the successful horse trainer – and this applies doubly to those engaged in bringing on polo ponies. At least 500 hours per mount are needed and with every horse an individual this entails many years of consistent work to develop a string of good playing animals. Cecil Smith is

Above ARGENTINE-STYLE HEAD COLLARS HELP THE INDIVIDUAL GROOM TO BRING THE STRING OF PONIES TO THE GAME. ***Right*** A WARM RELATIONSHIP DEVELOPS BETWEEN HORSE AND RIDER.

said never to have asked too much of a horse, and as the brilliant Juan Carlos Harriott, another 10-goaler, has said, when fatigue sets in then the first thing to go is the mind.

Both trainer and player must work hard to learn to rate a horse. One that is speed crazy may make brilliant runs but in the end will be of little use for providing a consistent mount on the polo field. The cultivation of the right attitude of the horse to its work is very important. Harold (Chico) Barry, who maintained a 9-goal rating for 15 years, counts the disposition of a pony as something to be specially looked at when choosing one. With the right disposition, he claims, a horse will make a good pony; without it there is no point in bothering with the animal.

If well-disposed towards the game, then with help from the rider a pony will learn to rate itself and give of itself fully without over-reaching and becoming a liability. Once this confidence has been learned, then other aspects of the game will be taught, such as not shying from the swishing of a polo stick, intelligently keeping to the play of the ball,

and being prepared to bump another pony. All these facets of obedience come with careful daily exercises designed for the purpose. Once taught the basics, the polo pony will be schooled in its weakest areas and when fully made it will need only enough work to keep it fit for the game.

Daily contact with his horses enables the player to learn to love and respect them and he soon notices problems and is able to deal with them. Also, both horse and rider need to learn to relax together. When the whistle is blown during a game this can be an important time for the conservation of energy and a thorough knowledge of the animal's condition and capabilities gained from regular exercising together will be a great asset. Claire Tomlinson, who plays at the highest level and is a top British breeder and trainer, like many others found that working on a ranch in South America has helped her work with horses. Riding all day, she says, means that you have to learn to relax on a horse and the resulting benefits to both training and playing are immeasurable.

Jack Williams

A welcome visitor in clubs throughout the world, and with a long and distinguished history in the game, including nine influential years as honorary polo manager at Cirencester Park Polo club, Jack Williams has done much for polo in many far-flung regions. He is typical of many whose love and expertise for polo have benefited scores of people — who in their turn are continuing the best traditions of the game.

Of great importance is his contribution towards the building up of the Sultan of Brunei's fabulous polo complex at Jerudong. The Royal Brunei Polo Club was born in the late 1970s when HRH the Sultan discovered the delights of the game. He asked Williams to select a string of polo ponies from Argentina and to take on the task of advising on technical aspects of setting up the club. In addition, Jack's teaching abilities were put to good use where members of the Brunei royal family and their retainers received expert tuition from him in the rudiments of the sport.

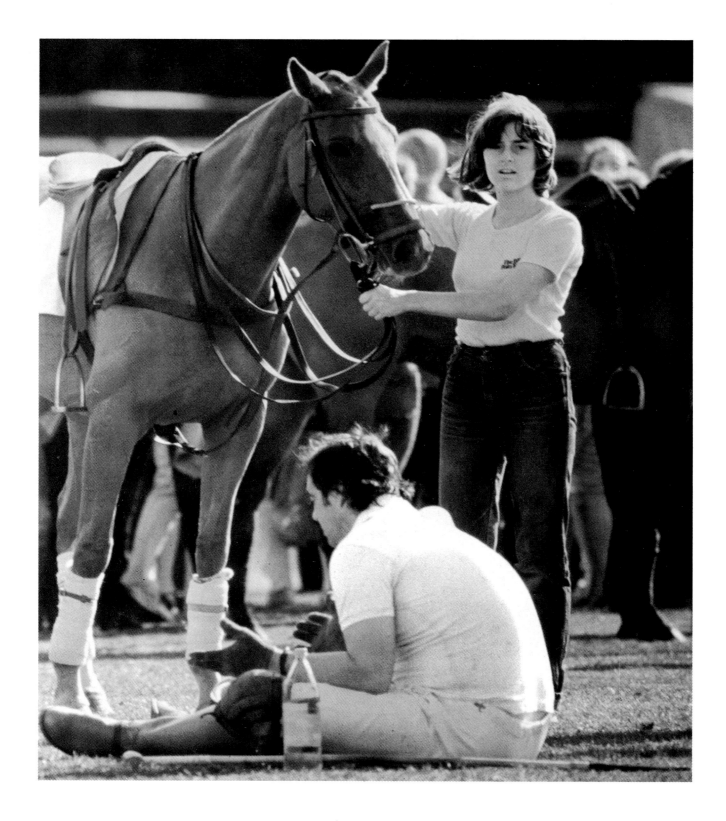

BOTH HORSE AND RIDER NEED A REST AFTER A
HARD-RIDDEN CHUKKA.

Different levels of the game of polo mean that green horses can be introduced gently to the play. Whatever its experience, it is important to leave any pony at the end of its chukka on a good note so that even if it has been fully extended it will be willing to return for the next match. Such things are learned by the rider and the benefits to the horse are evident in its performance.

At high-goal level a horse cannot be played for more than two or three months before being rested as the strains imposed are too great. Most, but not all, high-goal players keep their horses in during the playing season since it is important to harness their energies by stabling during the competitive period. Those who do not hold to this view suggest that, although they do not look as good if kept out, it is a more natural state for them to be in and therefore the ponies will be more relaxed. Turned out horses stay limber and healthy and need slightly less schooled exercise.

Whichever method is favoured, the ponies will be worked for a month before playing. For a week or two each one will be walked and trotted and then slow cantered until it is fit and in playing condition. It will then be worked hard galloping, walking, trotting, galloping on and off for at least an hour a day, with a further gentle walk again later. It should ideally be out of its stall at least two hours a day during the season but being played two or three times each week it is not usually thought necessary to gallop the pony much.

With such a strict and strenuous routine it will be seen that the groom has a big part to play and he or she must know as such about the pony as the player. Before going out for a chukka the pony ideally is worked for ten minutes or so by the groom and loosened up. He or she must also settle the animal so that it is properly ready to take its part in the game, and during chukkas the player should not have to worry about his ponies at all. Minor injuries must be treated at once and any others referred to the duty veterinarian. It is no longer regarded as necessary to "hot-walk" a horse when it comes off the field after its exertions, but a wash down and drying off are still needed – and this will be the responsibility of the groom.

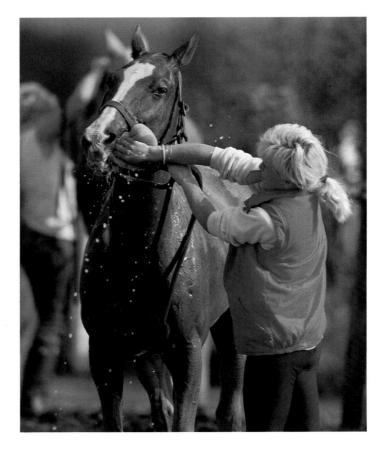

GROOMS ARE RESPONSIBLE FOR THE COMPLETE CARE OF THE PONIES, FROM EARLY MORNING EXERCISE (*right below*) TO COOLING THEM OFF AFTER A STRENUOUS GAME (*above*).

The rider's responsibilities towards the horse during play are to maintain a balanced easy seat and pace himself and his mount so that he can get the best from both of them, conserving energy when possible and extending to the limits when necessary. His control of his pony should be instinctive and his pony's actions extensions of his own. Aids to control usually include a whip – but rarely spurs. Only the occasional animal will need such harsh treatment and on the heels of the inexperienced in the heat of the game they can be far from kind. Billy Wayman suggests that spurs are best kept in the car for wearing in the bar after the match!

Tack for each horse is chosen to suit its particular needs. Sam Simonds of The Polo Shop in England and California and Tony Coppola of The Tackeria in Florida both specialise in polo equipment and between them they bring together most of the finest available for both polo pony and player. Saddles are available which have been part-designed by top players. Bridles and bits come in many shapes and sizes, with The Tackeria listing more than 100 bits and gags, the names of which often suggest their origin or those by whom they were favoured. The Argentine Roller Mouth Pelham (Coscojero), the Hitchcock gag, the Barry gag, the Balding (Half Moon) gag, the French Bradoon (Dr Bristol) are but a few of these.

All ponies are required to wear leg protection during a game and this practice is adhered to even when informal stick and balling takes place. Research has shown that wool and cotton bandages normally used will absorb some 7 per cent of a blow from a ball or stick. The other popular leg protector, the felt and leather boot, takes in approximately 14 per cent of the impact. A recently introduced lightweight plastic and polyurethane boot, developed by Anthony Porter and named after him, will absorb 27 per cent of the blow. The fact that Bristol University in England and individuals such as Porter are taking the trouble to research and develop polo equipment is a sign of the health of the sport and the general concern felt for the animals that make it so unique.

Above PRINCE CHARLES' ARGENTINIAN GROOM ENSURES THAT HIS NEXT MOUNT IS READY FOR HIM. *Right* IN ARGENTINA THE GAUCHO IS RESPECTED FOR HIS ABILITY AT WORKING HORSES.

Another reason for this concern is the increasing amounts of money being asked for trained and well-bred horses. The controversial American Peter Brant is thought by many to possess the best string of ponies outside of Argentina. This is not merely because he has a good eye and gets the best advice from the likes of the Pieres brothers who play in his team, but also because he is prepared to outbid others for the privilege of owning the most brilliant mounts. Brant is reputed to have said that he has spent more on just one of his famous racehorses than on a barn full of polo ponies – but many are beginning to doubt this as they enviously admire those bulging barns.

The price of polo ponies can vary from a couple of thousand to tens of thousands of dollars and perhaps the most money to be made in the game is by the buying and selling of horseflesh at the highest level. Many of the top players deal in the business of breeding or buying, making, playing and selling their ponies. There can be no better advertisement for an animal than for it to be seen ridden by a high-goal player in a series of winning matches, but this trade does inevitably cause problems for those engaged in it. Gonzalo Pieres expresses this difficulty when he tells of the need for a player to maintain the standard of his playing string and yet make money out of it. Selling gives him the means to afford to play at the highest level all over the world but by so doing he reduces the potential of the success which allows him to do just that.

The intense family polo rivalries that are fought out regularly during the Argentine Open tournaments are often seen in the building of the teams' horsepower. *Aficionados* will be heard along the pony lines and in the stands discussing the relative merits of the strings. Do the Heguys or the Pieres have the better horses? Who trains them best? Are they playing them in the correct order? Should the pony in the second chukka have been played against that marvellous horse played by the number 3 in the third? Surely that would have made more sense?

The decision as to which horse to play in what chukka is crucial. With a pattern in mind each player will discuss his line-up with his team-mates in the light of what is known about the opposition. Knowing the qualities and abilities of an opposing team's ponies is almost as useful as knowing about your own. The better mounts are often reserved for playing in what are referred to as the "fatal fourth" and the "crucial sixth" chukkas. Balancing the team's horsepower is important and if that can be matched with the qualities of the other side then so much the better. If a horse is to be played more than once in a game – and the best ones often are – then they tend to be played early

and late; perhaps the second and the sixth chukkas. Some players do not like doubling up their horses in this way. Indeed, Tommy Wayman reckons that the practice shortens by half the pony's playing life, a view that is not widely accepted.

When the Australian high-goal professional Ian (Ginger) Hunt married into the polo-playing Bamberg family in England, the patron of his team, Nicky Hahn, gave him a surprise wedding present which arrived at the reception wearing a big bow and four white leg bandages. It was a 10-year-old grey Australian gelding called Rio, a horse that had been played by Hunt and which had become a great favourite. Then and there, in the formal top hat and tails of his morning suit, he was persuaded to mount the pony for some stick and ball practice. For a polo player, said Ginger, there could be no better wedding present. And coming from a polo family his wife Clare readily agreed.

Lord Mountbatten used to delight in telling of an odd incident that happened in Hong Kong in 1922 when he was playing in the forward position on a Chinese pony and which might well stand as a tribute to the animal that makes the game possible. The ball was passed up to him and it hit the pony firmly underneath its tail. Clamping it down the horse is said to have galloped through the goal posts and calmly dropped the ball with a nonchalant lift of its tail.

In San Antonio, Texas, the Grea ranch, which is next door to the Retama Polo Center, has a sign over its entrance which reads: "Don't Want Nothin – But A Good Polo Pony" – a sentiment which all polo players will echo. Quite simply, the horse is *the* supreme being in the game.

HORSE AND RIDER – BOTH SUPREME ATHLETES.

A SEASON'S TOUGH PLAYING EXHAUSTS THE FITTEST PONIES. BUT KEPT
PROPERLY FIT AND CARED FOR, THEY SOON RECOVER FROM THEIR
EXERTIONS.

ALFONSO PIERES, WITH HIS 10-GOAL HANDICAP RATING, IS ABLE TO
NAME HIS PRICE WHEN PLAYING PROFESSIONALLY.

Money, Power
AND PATRONAGE

In Florida recently, the boss of an American beer company is rumoured to have spent $900,000 in 90 days on four high-goal polo teams. The operative word, of course, is "rumoured", because rumour is all that most people have to go on when money is mentioned in polo. The subject is often brought up, but rarely talked about in detail. In that way at least the old polo tradition remains that it is vulgar to discuss money. At its highest level nobody denies that it is an expensive game but how much it is costing an individual is very much his affair.

Things are changing, however, especially in America where – more than anywhere else – money is equated with power and it is not considered quite so sinful to flaunt it. Winning is important and to win one must have the best possible team. For that the highest prices must be paid. And, frankly, who cares about the rumours, just so long as they pitch the cash level higher – rather than lower – than it actually is!

The employment of professional players has long been an acceptable reality. It takes different forms, but the world's best can often command two "annual" salaries as they move between countries with the seasons. Those who employ them – the patrons – are the men and women who keep the game at a high-goal level. Without them the costs would be too high. In the countries of South America, however, there is a proud tradition which rejects local

professionalism, yet much of the game in these places relies on those players who travel and sell their services abroad.

At home, playing as amateurs amongst friends, the top South American players all tend to farm their own land and deal in horses. This lifestyle allows them to be comfortable – but not vastly rich. Riches come from horse dealing and playing abroad. Their skills, indicated by their playing handicap, can command high fees and will certainly ensure that their foreign travel and living expenses are paid for.

Until recently, the epithet "hired assassin" was often attached to the foreign professional. He fulfilled his patron's brief and allowed him at least to enjoy the game at a high level. Recently this pejorative tag is being dropped, perhaps as a true understanding of the role of the professional player is increasing. Although paid to be part of the team, the professional player's role, much as in the English household where there is a distinction between servants and staff, is more akin to that of the butler, nanny or estate manager. It is his job to make things happen as far as polo matters are concerned and ensure the general comfort of his master. But he also has privileges of confidence and friendship. He can tutor and admonish. He is trusted to take charge of the "family silver" as embodied in the horses.

His payment comes in many forms, with the most usual

being a deal which involves horses, expenses and fees. Some professionals are hired for a whole season – or even a whole year – working and playing for the same patron in more than one country. If not contracted to one patron only, a professional might play for different teams at different levels of the game. Whatever the arrangement, he will need to turn up on the field with the correct number of fit ponies prepared to play to win with his three team-mates. If he has the highest handicap he will most likely be expected to captain his side and be responsible for overall tactics and the play of the others. Many will also be responsible for the patron's horses, playing an important part in the running of the stables and the training of the mounts.

That an amateur – the patron – can so easily play alongside professionals is often a source of great wonder to those coming new to the game, and for the rich who want

to play polo, it may well be this aspect of the game that is one of its main attractions. Pro-am golf may give a taste but no other sport allows an amateur to buy his way in and play at the highest level. It is polo alone that can provide the "man who has everything" with that little bit more. The type of person who needs to win is the type who becomes a high-goal team patron.

While the professional is running the team, the patron needs to be generating the income to pay for it all. Even family money has to be maintained and those who start with such an advantage still have to work hard to keep what they have. Others get rich through a combination of talent, determination, and good fortune. When it comes to leisure activities they – like many others who are used to leading from the front in their business lives – want to enjoy their spare time in ways which are an extension of their business egos. If their money and power contribute greatly to putting together a top team involving the patron himself, then this is all part of the pleasure and satisfaction of polo.

Polo provides a sporting outlet for the rich businessman that is totally absorbing. During a game, every player needs one hundred per cent concentration and the concerns of the office cannot be brought on to the polo field. With a horse and seven other players to think about, all else is totally extraneous – even the insistent pleep of a car phone cannot be heard from the back of a galloping horse. Messages have to be taken by acolytes and relayed later, for nothing must interfere with the game. And those who do call requiring the boss's attention are likely to be suitably impressed when his secretary informs them that he cannot be contacted because he is on the polo field – the golf course pales into lazy insignificance by comparison. To the outside world, polo possesses a powerful and glamorous mystique and it does no harm at all to a man or woman's standing in the impressionable business world if it is known that their chosen sport is this fearless game.

Left HENRYK DE KWIATKOWSKI IS THE EPITOME OF THE FREE-SPENDING AMATEUR. HIS GREATEST LOVE IS TO PLAY WITH THE BEST IN THE WORLD IN HIS KENNELOT STABLES TEAM. *Right* HRH THE PRINCE OF WALES CHATTING WITH ESTÉE LAUDER (RIGHT). PRINCE CHARLES DOES MUCH TO ENCOURAGE THE SPONSORS WHICH HAVE BECOME SO NECESSARY FOR THE SURVIVAL OF THE SPORT.

Not all of those who are involved are players. Increasingly these days there are numerous opportunities for sponsorship and for the individual sponsors to enjoy a number of commercial advantages – not the least of which may be to shake the hand of a reigning monarch. The powerful are attracted by power and polo provides an ideal opportunity to display wealth and influence – and meet others who may help in its acquisition. Sponsorship takes a variety of forms, ranging from paying for a team to, more usually, financially backing a match or tournament. In between might be the simple buying of advertising space in a club programme or providing the prizes.

There has been an extraordinary growth in the number of commercial organisations prepared to put sponsorship money into the game, and the polo world still has an ambivalent attitude to this phenomenon. On the one hand many would like polo to remain the relaxed and exclusive sport that it once was; and on the other they recognise the need for sponsorship money to keep the game going. These two aspects need not be mutually exclusive but many polo people think that they are – especially in Britain.

Much of the change wrought by sponsorship is welcomed by everyone. A smart clubhouse in which to meet friends after the game is vastly superior to standing by the car in the sweltering sun or pouring rain sharing a drink. Well-plumbed lavatories have a distinct advantage over the nearest bush. The game can be better viewed from a comfortable stand. These are undoubted benefits which can be paid for by sponsorship money. Against these advantages can be balanced a loss of some of the intangibles that made polo such a special sport: an insouciant informality still found only a few years ago when one could attend a game and meet up with equals and friends without having to wear a badge to be recognised – and with none of the commercialism and overt hype generated by some, but certainly not all, sponsorship.

As always, the truth of the matter lies somewhere between the two extremes. With more men and women playing the game who increasingly demand a great degree of sophistication in their leisure surroundings, few are prepared to put up with an old wooden hut in the middle of a field in which to change. Claire Tomlinson, the world's highest-rated woman polo player, still tells of the time when she was obliged to shower with the genial Bertie Arbeid in order to be able to arrive at a post-polo engagement in a respectable condition. Men such as Arbeid can be guaranteed to remain gentlemen under any circumstances, but the fact is that sponsorship money can mean the difference between semi-squalor and modern amenities.

A large polo club requires a great deal of finance for its day-to-day running; on public days the ground and office staff need complementing with stewards; and general maintenance can also be costly. Players' fees are supplemented by sponsorship money and many a low-goal player is able to continue in the game only because his club fee is not prohibitive. On the downside, the loss of intimacy brought about by the introduction of sponsorship can be very real – especially when members of the Royal Family or film and TV celebrities are in attendance. The lure of meeting a public figure can attract many guests and in addition members of the general public are more likely to attend a match if they think they can achieve the double thrill of watching an exciting polo match *and* spotting celebrities. Inevitably this means the imposing of restrictions. For instance, the job of the grooms would be made impossible if large crowds were

allowed to wander into the pony lines.

The returns on a polo sponsorship investment are often difficult to calculate. A lot of publicity can be gained because the media worldwide are increasingly willing to cover the sport and make mention of those who back it – which can pay dividends to a commercial organisation wanting to be seen in a marketplace regarded as the exclusive preserve of the rich. Just as useful as press coverage, though, is the unique entertainment value of polo. A beautiful, fast and exciting aristocratic game which takes place in superb and spacious settings provides an excellent backdrop for corporate entertaining on a lavish scale.

Top customers of the sponsor, colleagues and even senior members of the workforce can all be comfortably accommodated on the edges of the polo field and entertained in luxuriously appointed marquees. Company heads can sit with special guests in the place of honour and be part of the proceedings by presenting the prizes. The likelihood in the UK of making a presentation to the heir to the throne – or with Her Majesty the Queen alongside – offers an added bonus. Even in monarch-free countries, polo possesses that unique type of magnetism that attracts many celebrities who enhance the status of the event by their presence.

Left THE ANNUAL PATRONS MATCH AT THE ROYAL BERKSHIRE CLUB IS PROBABLY
THE ONLY TIME THAT MANY OF THESE MEN PLAY WITH THEIR PEERS AND
WITHOUT PROFESSIONALS TO BACK THEM UP.
THE INVOLVEMENT OF THOSE FEATURED FREQUENTLY BY THE MEDIA IS AN ADDED
ATTRACTION TO THE GAME OF POLO. PRINCE CHARLES (***below***) AND ACTRESS
STEPHANIE POWERS (***above***), WITH SOCIETY PORTRAIT PAINTER VIK ADVANI,
BOTH PLAY THE GAME ALL OVER THE WORLD.

Far left THE PRINCESS OF WALES CHATS TO REGULAR DISABLED POLO GROUPIE JOHN PRESTWICH AND HIS WIFE MAGGIE. ALTHOUGH UNABLE TO MOVE, HE IS STILL ABLE TO ENJOY THE UNIQUE EXCITEMENT OF THE GAME. *Left below* THE RAISED SCOREBOARD PROVIDES AN IDEAL VANTAGE POINT FROM WHERE TO VIEW THE GAME.

Above left THE QUEEN MAKES A PRESENTATION TO SPONSOR ALFRED DUNHILL AFTER A GAME AT WINDSOR. *Above right* THE PRINCESS OF WALES AND MAJOR RONALD FERGUSON TALK TO SPONSOR'S GUESTS AFTER A GAME. *Below* GUESTS ARRIVE AT A POLO MATCH AFTER AN AFTERNOON'S RACING AT ROYAL ASCOT.

It is in Deauville, France, each year during the month of August, that aspects of polo money, power and patronage are at their most overt. Begun in 1950 by François André, owner of the fashionable casino, the Coupe d'Or polo tournament attracts Europe's top high-goal teams and the whole month is given over to polo, racing, and other forms of high living. Only the "seriously rich" can afford to be there and despite a good local airport for jetting in and out, real commitment is needed to stay the course.

It has been estimated that a patron must put aside at least $100,000 in order to enjoy the month at Deauville with his family, friends and polo team. The town is *en fête*, the hotels are full and the casino bustling. Money flows out like the nearby River Seine into the sea. August in Deauville is the place to be and a conspicuous celebration of both horse and human flesh is there to be enjoyed by all who can afford it – or by those with coveted polo skills.

Human flesh in all its variegated shapes and sizes is much in evidence on the beach or by the hotel swimming pools; casual chic is the general order of dress in other places. Horseflesh attracts many buyers to the important annual sale of yearlings which takes place during the month. Besides the polo, Deauville's main race meetings take place during August and so in the streets to the south of the town horses are as much in evidence as people. Racing and polo stables are dotted around the racecourse and polo ground, which is in the middle of the Hippodrome de la Touques.

It is at Deauville that patrons and team managers often begin to make their assessments. The world's best players are all present, sure that here they will meet their peers and be seen by the patrons who may employ them in the future. Winning ways are noted and fees discussed. Deals may not be made there and then but talk tends to be all about the game and much useful information is gained. Deals which have been struck ready for the next season are rumoured about and commented upon. Is that 9-goaler really worth such a fee? Will that playing combination work? Were those horses bought for rather too much money or did the buyer see something in them that others did not? Performances in the casino might indicate considerable wealth and often show a recklessness of spirit that will later win games on the polo field. With little else but leisure between matches, there is plenty of time for gossip, conversation, and conjecture.

Most people involved with polo stay at the Hotel Royal, which provides a comfortable and expansive meeting place. While chauffeurs and nannies look after the domestic side of life, patrons, their wives and girlfriends, can enjoy being with their polo-playing friends and the professionals they employ.

Many of the South American professional players at Deauville, besides receiving expenses and a salary, may also agree to purchase, ship and train a number of horses for a fixed price which will supplement their earnings and at the same time provide the patron with the means of mounting himself and others who will join the team. Deauville is the ideal place to firm up such details – and to enjoy many of life's rich pleasures.

AT DEAUVILLE, MRS PIERRE TARI AND FLORENCE AND CATHERINE MACAIRE ARE ON THEIR HOME GROUND.

The location of a polo club is becoming increasingly important when sponsorship and public support are so necessary for the continued survival of the game at its highest levels. The days of the private club are by no means numbered, but a means of marketing those that need outside support to survive is now considered essential.

A location which links the field with a related sporting or social activity can certainly be useful. Deauville's polo, like many others, is linked with horseracing. As in the Indian city of Calcutta, the grounds are in the middle of the racecourse and, again as with Ascot and Goodwood in England, polo tournaments are associated with the premier race meetings. Moving effortlessly from the racetrack to the polo field is especially pleasurable to those out to enjoy a day's entertainment from horses.

That the Guards Polo Club in England is in the Royal Windsor Great Park underneath the Queen's castle home and very near to Ascot where some of the world's best horseracing takes place is no mere accident. Windsor is within easy striking distance of London, the capital city. The Household Division, the Queen's personal bodyguard, are stationed in both places and they form the backbone of the club's playing members. The beautiful parkland setting is ideal and sponsors are glad of the opportunity to come into the Queen's "back garden" and

to be able to meet there members of her family and many of her subjects.

Beautiful locations – though perhaps less convenient – are also the attraction of two other of England's most important polo clubs. The Earl Bathurst's Gloucestershire country estate of Cirencester Park and the Viscount Cowdray's Sussex home, Cowdray Park, both allow visitors to enjoy the particular delights of the English countryside and provide an ideal location for a day out. Members of the general public are welcomed and consequently help to provide for better club facilities by paying entrance fees. At these enchanting places – previously the preserve of the aristocracy and their circle – sponsors are pleased to undertake their corporate entertaining.

One of England's newest and most successful polo clubs enjoys the best of both worlds. The Royal County of Berkshire Polo Club was created on the site of a former racing stables close to Ascot racecourse and is just down the road from the Guards club. An exclusively private club, it only welcomes members of the general public on particular sponsored days. The club is presided over by its joint owners Bryan Morrison and Norman Lobel, both also patrons of high-goal teams. The club employs a group of professionals who undertake both to instruct and play

AMERICAN PATRONS GEORGE SHERMAN JR AND PAUL BUTLER OF OAK BROOK.

with members and all facilities are of the highest quality. The true spirit of entrepreneurship is much in evidence and as well as polo the Royal Berkshire offers such sports as squash, tennis, real tennis and croquet.

The enterprise shown by the founders of the Royal County of Berkshire club is not too common in the UK – but in the USA it is an acknowledged concomitant for success and throughout America new clubs have been founded upon similar lines. Often based on the development of real estate for home, holiday and business accommodation, the polo club is made the central feature of a complex which provides for the total recreational needs and desires of the community. At such places as Palm Beach in Florida, Oak Brook near Chicago, and Santa Barbara in California, there have arisen splendid and successful polo clubs which are well patronised by both players and spectators.

While retaining a certain exclusivity, the public profile of such clubs is high and socially they are as much a success as they are from a sporting point of view, attracting international players and massive sponsorship. Those

running them, the Butler family at Oak Brook, for example, are important local figures serving their community in many different ways. They enjoy their wealth conspicuously but such is their contribution to those around them and to their polo clubs that this is not resented. In fact, the local community usually benefits considerably from the influx of high-spending newcomers and visitors.

In South America – where the living is cheaper – the sport is regarded in an entirely different light. For instance, in Argentina, where most of the clubs are situated around Buenos Aires, polo is played frequently and regularly at home on the *estancia*, the clubs providing meeting places for families involved in the game at weekends. Here the standards are higher than anywhere else in the world and opportunities for improving playing skills and ponies are immense. Because there are no patrons with low handicaps on the ground the games are faster and more dashing. The amateur status of the game is a source of pride and men expect to meet their equals on the field of play. Those on the sidelines who are not playing have an extraordinary knowledge of the sport and its stars. They possess an in-depth understanding of the players and their best horses and when it comes to the playing of the Argentine Open at the end of November a huge crowd comes together to appreciate the finest play that the world of polo can offer. Commentary by public address – common in Europe and the US – is unnecessary: most around the field know exactly what is going on.

In South America, where the handicap of all the teams involved far exceeds that which is even allowed in high-goal polo in most other countries, there is much to appreciate. All this talent is nurtured at home and in the small country clubs in which the best qualifications are horsemanship and ability with the stick and ball. Many people elsewhere in the world would also like these to be the only criteria, but outside of South America the possession of social skills can often stand a polo player in better stead.

In Australasia, polo clubs offer probably the widest spread of styles, the South American farm model existing alongside the European and North American type club. Land and horses are cheaper and more plentiful so polo tends to have an appeal for those involved in farming and comes more naturally than to those raised and earning their wealth in the cities. However, money earned in the cities of the world is coming into Australian polo in a big way. Kerry Packer, who made his sporting name transforming and commercialising cricket, has taken to polo and is putting his considerable resources into its development as a mass-appeal sport.

The price of horses in Australia and New Zealand has risen within the past few years – in direct proportion to the number of animals that Packer has been buying. He has engaged the services of the best local players and offered secure and attractive backing to members of his new team. As with so many like him in the game he throws his weight fully behind his involvement and demands and gets the same amount of loyalty and hard work that he himself puts in. Within only a few years he has joined the gallery of other super-patrons, like Peter Brant of America, Galen Weston of Canada, Guy Wildenstein of France, Alex Ebeid of Egypt and the Yeomans of England, who have spent fortunes on maintaining winning top-rated teams capable of outrunning the best.

CANADIAN GALEN WESTON IS A GENEROUS INTERNATIONAL PATRON OF POLO. HIS MAPLE LEAF TEAM HONOURABLY FLIES THE FLAG FOR HIS COUNTRY WHEREVER IT PLAYS.

Motives for polo involvement are never clear, but being the best seems to feature high on the list, this aspect remaining an important factor in the continuing of polo in the army. Demonstrating power is an important emotional need and, as has so often been the case in the past, when men are not at war then sporting achievement can be a useful substitute for proving superiority. In India the officers of the 61st Cavalry play for the honour of the regiment, even though their fellows in other units no longer continue the game. As the last remaining fully-mounted active cavalry regiment, members of the 61st do not have a great deal to do, so playing polo in various centres around the country allows them to show the flag, maintain active skills of horsemanship and regularly exercise the aggressive qualities which go for making good soldiers.

The cavalry regiments in England have just as proud a tradition to maintain and do so with the active encouragement of the Establishment. If the Colonel-in-Chief and heir to the throne plays, then there can be no

finer inspiration. Young officers in the Guards particularly, but also in the Hussars and other regiments, are offered cheap instruction and hire of horses at very reasonable rates. The various army competitions, the Inter-Regimental and Captains and Subalterns matches, for example, are fiercely contested. It has even been known for a particularly useful playing officer to be found duties in the United Kingdom while his unit is serving abroad – in order that he could be included in a team.

Above MAJOR KULDEEP GARCHA OF THE INDIAN 61ST CAVALRY IS A POPULAR INTERNATIONAL PLAYER.

MRS HELEN BOEHM WITH "HER BOYS", TWO PAIRS OF HIGH-GOAL
BROTHERS: JULIAN HIPWOOD, CARLOS GRACIDA, MEMO GRACIDA AND HOWARD HIPWOOD.

Even if a patron's team does not win, and there are some who rarely succeed – despite the money spent on putting them together – there is definitely a sense of superiority to be gained from "owning" a polo team, even if the sheer physical aspect is immense. Shared teams do exist but they are just as high profile as any other and the question of who pays for what need never be discussed outside of the family.

An efficient yard run by a manager and a team of grooms must be found close to the home polo club. It must be easily accessible as it is essential for everybody who plays the game to practise "stick and ball" and to ride as often as possible. In practice this means that players usually have a home nearby, if the yard is not actually an integral part of the property. Some professional players own all their own horses, and some none, so besides the horses that he rides himself, the patron must have mounts which he can lend to other members of the team.

A quarter of a million dollar bill for the putting together

and maintaining of a high-goal team for a season is not unusual. There will probably be at least 30 polo ponies in any yard, being cared for if not owned by the patron. A reliable transport system needs to be maintained for all the horses. Games are likely to be played away from the home club and the yard itself may not be within easy riding distance of the field, even if games are played locally. The visiting foreign professional will often be provided with both accommodation and transport during his stay so that, too, adds to the general complement. With so many animals veterinary and farrier bills are regular and high. Feed bills and a tremendous amount of equipment for both horse and player which has to be regularly replaced are other financial burdens. Polo exists in a generous and social world and the entertainment costs to a patron can also mount up considerably during a season.

There is no set cost for hiring professionals, and it is certainly possible to find a useful foreign player who will help win games but not be vastly expensive. At least one top American patron is renowned for bringing brilliant young, unknown South American players with a comparatively low handicap (and therefore low price tag) into the country for their first year. When the US Polo Association puts up such a player's handicap to a more realistic level at the end of the season, he has already served his patron's purposes. He returns the following year – but at a higher price and to a different patron.

This highlights an aspect of polo that is rarely discussed. Individual handicap levels are very important for the making of a team when there is a limit on the level of play. With a usual top limit of 22 goals for high-goal polo the correct combination of players is vital and their choosing a great art. Handicaps are changed at the end of each season and contracts and agreements cannot be finally made until the changes are known. Thus there is a period when scheming becomes both necessary and essential if the following year's team is to stand any chance of success. Loyalties are strong but a handicap change up or down can affect the composition of a team and players have to be dropped and new ones taken on to get the balance right.

Opinions as to the suitability of a particular handicap are bound to differ. Players are watched by many throughout the season and the decision is never one person's, although rumours fly every so often that the handicap committee has been "persuaded" in its deliberations over certain players. It is quite a subjective affair, but on the whole the system does work and the general objective of producing teams of roughly equal ability is usually achieved.

From the earliest days of polo there have been differing rules and regulations about matters within the game. For example, it is still the case that a player can have a particular handicap in one country and a higher or lower one in another. The problems thrown up by these differences are not often severe, but in such an international game they should not really exist. Many in the game recognise a need for consistency and the formation of the International Polo Federation is the latest and most effective attempt to bring together all polo-playing countries under one system of regulation. It has many problems to solve but it is doing much to encourage the sort of international competition that can be truly recognised as indicating national abilities. It is also attempting to have polo reinstated as an Olympic sport.

However, despite its good intentions, the IPF has not managed to persuade all nations to join the federation, the British Hurlingham Polo Association being the most notable absentee. The banning of Argentinian players from British competition following the Falklands crisis has also been a great stumbling block to international co-operation. Yet the British position has begun to soften and the Argentinians have returned in 1989. Hopefully, the global position will be reconsidered sooner rather than later and a truly international organization will evolve.

THE MOMENT OF VICTORY IS SWEET FOR THE PATRON WHO WILL HAVE SPENT MUCH MONEY AND FOUGHT HARD TO WIN. RONALDO DE LIMA FROM BRAZIL POPS THE CHAMPAGNE.

Left MEXICAN 10-GOALER CARLOS GRACIDA. *Right* ARGENTINE OPEN, 1988. LEFT TO RIGHT: MARCOS URANGA, ROBERTO CAVANAGH, AND ROBERTO DE VICENZO. *Below* THE TROPHIES FOR THE ARGENTINE OPEN, POLO'S MOST COVETED PRIZES.

BRYAN MORRISON DISCUSSES POLO WITH HIS PARTNER NORMAN LOBEL.

BRYAN MORRISON

O F HIS MULTI-MILLION-DOLLAR private polo club in the Royal County of Berkshire, Bryan Morrison declares: "It's not a business, it's a piece of art. It's a personal thing which instead of being on the wall is out there." And with an expansive wave of his cigar he sweeps an arm in the general direction of the luxurious spread which has taken him and his partner Norman Lobel only a few short years to take from dreams to reality.

A man of impeccable style, with roots in the music business, publishing such superstars as Pink Floyd and George Michael, Morrison had a great vision for his club and within three years he has seen that fulfilled with a vengeance. With six grounds, tennis courts, a croquet lawn and plans for many more amenities surrounding the splendid clubhouse and stabling for 200 horses, the Royal County of Berkshire Polo Club has become an irresistible social magnet. Polo, however, is the club's raison d'être and most of the partying – of which there seems to be an inordinate amount – comes from the various members' love of life.

Morrison eschews the second rate. He is always at the centre of activity, enthusiastically determined to ensure that every detail contributes to polo perfection. Chairs and iced water for thirsty players will be found in the pony lines, non-playing wives and girlfriends will always find some activity within the club to occupy them. This is the ultimate polo environment designed exclusively by a master for playing members and their guests.

Bryan Morrison and Norman Lobel have formed their own dream polo community within a marvellous park setting. And their impact on other English clubs is immense. The Royal County of Bershire Polo Club caters for the new generation of polo players, stars of stage, screen and the pop world – as well as captains of industry – for whom only the best is acceptable. So no longer is a wooden hut in the middle of the field considered tolerable. Today polo players and their guests demand something a little special . . .

A source of great pleasure to Bryan Morrison is the fact that his son Jamie has taken to the game. A young teenager, he has quietly been taking instruction and already is proving a useful addition to his father's team. And to think that it was only a few years ago that he ran up to Bryan during an afternoon's polo at the Royal Berkshire and asked, "Daddy, is it true what they say that you *own* this club?" Such is the charm of this polo enthusiast and his family.

Left THE EXPANSIVE BRYAN MORRISON ALWAYS SEEMS TO BE ENJOYING HIMSELF ON THE POLO FIELD. *Below* TYPICALLY, MORRISON HAS NOT FORGOTTEN THOSE WHO ENCOURAGED HIM IN HIS EARLY DAYS AND HIS OLD MENTOR, BILLY WALSH, WHO DID MUCH TO REVIVE THE GAME AFTER THE LAST WAR, IS COMMEMORATED IN THE BERKSHIRE CLUB BY HAVING A FIELD NAMED AFTER HIM. *Right* LOS MACHOS, THE ROCKSTAR TEAM OF MIKE RUTHERFORD (GENESIS), KENNY JONES (THE WHO), AND BRYAN MORRISON, WITH STUART COPELAND (THE POLICE). *Below right* GRETA MORRISON (LEFT) AND ALISON LOBEL (RIGHT) PICTURED AT THEIR HUSBANDS' BERKSHIRE CLUB WITH HELEN BOEHM (CENTRE).

Left THE MAYOR OF DEAUVILLE, COMTESSE ANNE D'ORNANO.
Below JEAN-LUC CHARTIER, THE ELEGANT FRENCH POLOIST.

JEAN-LUC CHARTIER

Parisian lawyer jean-luc chartier practises a brilliant career, but it is probably in the world of polo that he is best known. Author of the lavish book *Polo de France*, he has an elegance and personal style which epitomise the tournament for which he is the organiser.

Deauville in Normandy is *the* place to be in Europe during the month of August for the major celebration of the horse, which centres on racing and polo. The Championnat Mondial de Polo, which has taken place every year since 1950, attracts the best and the richest players from all over the world and it is the immensely charming Monsieur Chartier who presides over the smooth running of the tournament. High sporting and social traditions are maintained at Deauville and they require careful nurturing by Chartier and his team, backed by the Comtesse Anne D'Ornano, Mayor of the town, and such as M. Philippe Gazagne, Director General of the Societé des Hôtels et Casino de Deauville – employer of 1,200 people in a place with a population of 5,000.

Jean-Luc Chartier is typical of a particular type of amateur in the game of polo. Any lack of financial gain does not mean a lack of standards and both as a player and an administrator, he works as hard as in any of his professional ventures. His love of the game began after the showjumping club of which he was a member disbanded and he was introduced by Claude Terrail to the polo school run by Jaques Macaire at the Bagatelle club in Paris. Soon after that he was playing for Guy Wildenstein's Diables Bleus team, which enjoyed great success in France, Britain and throughout Europe. Now another Macaire, the top-rated French player Lionel, joins him regularly in the organisation of the Deauville tournament and Chartier has followed Wildenstein as president of the Association Sportive du Polo de Deauville.

"Courage, endurance, submission, discipline, calmness, judgement, speed of observation and *sang-froid* are what makes polo the king of sports after having been for so long the sport of kings," says Chartier. "As grand a spectacle today as it was yesterday, polo is sport *par excellence*; without doubt it is perfectly adapted to those qualities essential to the horseman."

MEMO GRACIDA, 10-GOALER AND MEMBER OF THE FAMOUS
MEXICAN POLO-PLAYING DYNASTY.

8

AMERICAN POLO
A PERSONAL VIEW
FRANK ROHR

THE
PIMM'S BOOK OF
POLO

Y ou couldn't comfortably drink champagne from the engraved, embossed 27-inch-high silver ewer with its handhold of rearing polo ponies. But many high-goalers have tried, and not a few have supped both bubbly and the purer stuff of realized dreams from this historic US Open trophy.

On 25 September 1988, before a cheering crowd of 5,000, 10-goaler Memo Gracida of the winning Diables Bleus team held aloft the 84-year-old symbol of the premier triumph in US polo. He'd won the first-ever US Open series held at the tournament's new home in the Lexington Horse Park of Kentucky under the aegis of the United States Polo Association, now permanently ensconced at this 1,000-acre bluegrass haven.

After a week of rain, the brand new Man-O'-War Field wasn't exactly fast as fire but expert drainage and benign delay made it eminently playable for eight superstars of polo in Camelot weather for the recharged Open. Together with three other US polo "firsts" at Lexington – the new C. V. Whitney Cup for the Handicap Division of the Open, the inauguration of the Museum of Polo and Hall of Fame, and the renewal of the prestigious Westchester Cup – the occasion gave to players, patrons and pundits US polo in crucible for the 80s and beyond.

There were the masterly moguls: top-ranked Mexican and Argentine professionals, gallant US peers, celebrities and their retinues, magnetised media and a new wave of astute sponsors who discern in polo's gutsy glamour a quality linkage where, like the goals, the styles are high and the blood is blue, and – as they are discovering – the bottom line is black.

Since the early 1970s, there's been a rompin' stompin' rebirth of the Game of Kings in the US. In media sectors, polo is politely galloping onto sports pages, fashion layouts and TV screens across the country. Allan Scherer, new Executive Director of the USPA, says, "Today we have over 2,600 registered USPA members and 250 active clubs. We've seen a greater membership growth within the past two years than ever in the history of American polo." This means a 45 per cent membership rise in the past six years and a 52 per cent increase in clubs, not including 21 colleges with polo facilities.

The good life at fieldside on the day of the '88 Open – new role model for upscale clubs from Palm Beach to Palm Springs – makes it easy to see why. In the Gold Section pavilion, moored just astern of the preferred grandstand, uniformed butlers stand sentinel. It's almost game time as guests come sauntering in from an outdoor Pimm's Chukker reception to their luncheon festival of hauteur, horsemanship and discreet hype. These folks are ageless, animated, tanned. Dress code is blazer and tie, linen suit and real jewellery. On field, a four-in-hand coach carries the likes of "aristocrat" Marylou Whitney, veteran poloist and Thoroughbred owner, Leverett Miller and the Rajmata of Jaipur.

As the Culver Academy Mounted Black Horse Troop performs, ardent sunshine turns the playing field banknote green: Bermuda grass will do that in certain lights. In the tent's alcove, a combo plays Nöel and Cole. To an obligato of popping champagne corks, eight world-class Open finalists materialise at midfield: French art tycoon Guy Wildenstein's Diables Bleus and S. ("Skeeter") Johnston III's Coca-Cola team. You feel the energy in the mix of sporting bloods, society beauties, tailgating swells, high-goal champions and low-flying ponies.

The Channel silhouette of Allan's wife Margaret Scherer floats in and out of frame, putting the finishing touches to her finely tuned party, best of the polo season. In the serendipitous fashion of US family polo, Maggy Scherer, via her own company Palm Beach Directions, is producing the event for guests and the Open's first-time corporate backers: title sponsor Toyota and team and participating Open sponsor Coca-Cola. Toyota's equally gala tent is pitched 50 yards downfield.

The horn sounds at midfield; the ball is dropped; the 1988 US Open starts. Inevitably it evokes a comment by playwright Philip (*Philadelphia Story*) Bary: "The prettiest sight in this fine pretty world is the privileged class enjoying its privileges." That enjoyment filters down vigorously to the grass roots bear-and-pretzels poloists, says Scherer, who now comprise the fastest-growing sector of the US polo community.

To box the polo compass from northeast, midsouth and Florida to Texas, Illinois and California, is to scan its grandest venues and derive from their unsparing stylists and players polo's growing dynamism and its new directions on the sporting scene.

Obvious, of course, is the new USPA polo headquarters in the Horse Park of Lexington, Kentucky, where in one year of planning and production four brand new polo fields were built, "And three more are in construction," says Allan Scherer. In this first of three contracted years for the Open to remain at Lexington, a crowd of 5,000 watched two of the world's six 10-goalers – legendary Mexican brothers Carlos and Memo Gracida – help their patron Guy Wildenstein and his Diables Bleus with Terry Moore of Oklahoma triumph 11-8 over the opposing 26-goal squad of Coca-Cola, captained by Skeeter Johnston III of Tennessee whose team included Argentine 10-goaler

(9 in the US) Marcos Heguy, fellow Argentine Ernesto Astrada and Jeff Atkinson of Tennessee.

There was a traditional, terrible beauty in the hard-fought game and a new Kentucky ambience that spoke encouragingly to visiting polo principals like Skeeter's father Summerfield K. ("Skey") Johnston, Jr., former USPA Chairman. "It's a great point of pride for us to bring the US Open to the new fields of Kentucky Horse Park," said Skey. "It has to have an inspirational effect on US polo; a lot of eyes will open to the sport; sponsors may throng; and TV may yet learn how to cover polo as it deserves." One optimistic caveat comes from Skey: "If

polo at the Horse Park proves as popular as we anticipate, the USPA may later consider splitting the event into two divisions with one for the West Coast."

In swift and sparkling succession at Lexington, Man-O'-War Field hosted the inaugural C.V. Whitney Cup as Handicap Division of the two-tiered Open, and the first revival of the England-US Westchester Cup competition since 1939.

On hand to present his namesake cup was C.V. "Sonny" Whitney himself, renowned three-time winner of the Open itself in 1928, 1937 and 1938. "My biggest win was in '37 against my own cousin Jock Whitney and Tommy Hitchcock," said C.V. as the first namesake match wound down to a 15-10 victory by Fort Lauderdale over Boca Raton. "That was my greatest triumph until I went into the movie business and married Marylou who was starring in my picture *Missouri Troubles*."

As for the Open's new venue: "This is a grand go-ahead home for the Open," said C.V. whose own Lexington estate has now become a major trophy source for the new Museum of Polo. Marylou, she of the blonde cut-crystal looks and high-goal enthusiasm, stamped down divots at the half and then shored up C.V.'s recollections as she explained how she was literally making free with the

Whitney memorabilia: "I'm giving all our trophies to the Museum, except those I use for water pitchers. They can be so handy. The rest belong properly to the Museum, which is like giving them to all our friends in the community of polo."

Marylou also passed a deserved palm to high-goalers Will Farish, another Horse Park polo devotee, and Greenwich Polo Club founder Peter Brant who had helped the Whitneys revive Saratoga polo in the mid-70s on the same field C.V.'s grandfather had built for his son Harry Payne Whitney. Polo does have its working aristocracy, never more evident than when they themselves rejuvenate its heritage.

Left FRENCH ART DEALER GUY WILDENSTEIN IS USED TO WINNING. HE IS SEEN HERE WITH THE US OPEN CUP. *Above* C.V. AND MARYLOU WHITNEY CONGRATULATE ERNESTO TROTZ ON HIS WINNING OF THE C.V. WHITNEY CUP.

JOHN OXLEY OF BOCA RATON WITH HIS SON JACK. STILL PLAYING IN HIS 80TH
YEAR, JOHN IS THE OLDEST HIGH-GOAL PLAYER IN THE WORLD.

Captain of the winning Fort Lauderdale Team for the C.V. Whitney Cup was Jack Oxley whose rival the Johnny Walker Boca Raton team featured Jack's own remarkable 79-year-old father John T. Oxley, oldest and still most daunting active member of the USPA. Son Jack, who is new USPA chairman, had nothing but praise for the dramatic USPA construct: "A grand presence with top players. Best polo news since my father and I together won the English Gold Cup over there in 1970."

Aristocracy from the subcontinent of India graced the first of two days on which the revived Westchester Cup was played. The '88 schedule for this renowned trophy was 2 and 9 October between a US foursome and, thanks to a standoff with Old Blighty herself, an Australasia team led by Jaime McKay, who wore the requisite Commonwealth colours and lost on a net point basis to the Americans captained by Bart Evans.

High drama and also high romance enlivened the first game, thanks to a new Jaipur Cup created for the USPA by the convivial Maharaja of Jaipur, Colonel Sawai Bhawani Singh – "Bubbles" to his friends, who use the sobriquet given the infant Maharaja when his arrival as the first male heir in two generations so delighted his royal parents they filled an Olympic-sized palace swimming pool with champagne. Bubbles presented his new Jaipur Cup as programmed to the American winners of the first day of the Westchester series.

Right MARCOS URANGA, PRESIDENT OF THE INTERNATIONAL POLO FEDERATION.

THE LEADING LIGHTS BEHIND THE POLO MUSEUM AND HALL OF FAME:
CHAIRMAN PHILIP IGLEHART AND DIRECTOR OF OPERATIONS LINDA BESADE.

The premier event of the spacious and handsomely endowed Museum of Polo which had directly followed the finals of the 1988 US Open was hosted by its chairman, revered polo historian and former 7-goaler Philip Iglehart, along with museum board member and muse Linda Besade. The ambitious goal of this permanent and acquisition-minded Polo Museum, the first of its kind in the world says Philip Iglehart, is "To educate the general US public to the sport of polo, to create artistic theatre for polo's imperishable artefacts."

Where did this former Meadow Brook champion and now self-appointed polo chronicler get his archival drive? "Linda pushed me," smiles Philip.

Sharing celebratory Moët on that golden afternoon with Museum guests was Argentine high-goaler Marcos Uranga, now president of the International Polo Federation representing players in 25 nations and stager of polo's world championships. Señor Uranga, longtime contender on the US high-goal circuit from Palm Beach to Santa Barbara, had a prescient comment on the new USPA Lexington venture: "It's fantastic for the USPA to be set now in its own fields . . . so encouraging for the growth of

American polo whose level is getting closer and closer to our own."

Enjoying the reception with Sr. Uranga was an American whose level had always been dangerously close to the Argentine supernovas: William T. Ylvisaker. Among acknowledged kings of the splendid strife that is high-goal polo, Bill Ylvisaker's place as USPA seer and peerless competitor is unassailable. His lifetime role in polo as both selfless custodian and steely innovator is simply greater than the sum of its parts. In the ideal sense, it combines anticipation, the quality most prized by Ylvisaker in a match, and response. Both are evident in comments on the new Lexington home for the USPA: "The Lexington venue is ideal; so is the timing of its September schedule. I'd hope this would one day become the premier tournament of US polo. All that's needed now is an increase in the number of teams. And that should come."

Ylvisaker's inner polo field, like the track he's on, is fast as fire. The real heat is evident, however, and so is the light when after a typical game you see the former 7-goaler cradling a silver trophy in the winner's circle. If you would know the age, the elation of this game of kings, look into the face of this polo athlete after a match in the lee of the bunting and the tenting. It's all there in the glinting hazel gaze, the cheeks hollowed by a draining game, brow glistening with the high-priced glory of six grinding chukkas.

Now an electronics industry leader whom *Fortune* magazine once included among "The Ten Toughest Bosses", Ylvisaker served as USPA Governor back in 1959, and Chairman from '69 to '75. In those days, he burnished a polo dream which he fulfilled in 1977. As then CEO of Gould, Inc., he broke ground in West Palm Beach on 1,650 acres of Wellington swampland that he transformed with astonishing dispatch into Palm Beach Polo and Country Club. Even as the USPA rating system takes the measure of a man's polo talent, the PBPCC today is the standard by which all world-class polo centres are judged. The multi-million-dollar PBPCC sports/equestrian complex maintains 11 Bermuda grass fields, stabling for more than 1,000 horses, and superb golf, tennis, squash and croquet for the unmounted within a luxurious landscape of private villas, condominiums and clubhouses.

In 1987, as Ylvisaker moved on to new corporate and polo challenges, his nation-state among polo resorts was cordially acquired by the California-based Landmark Land Company whose president, Chris Cole, has come forward as an enthusiastic polo supporter. With all 11 fields in use, the Ylvisaker legacy is lively throughout the January–May high-goal season. Top teams from more

than 20 countries compete for cups that became world-class prizes during the first dazzling of PBPCC, such as the $100,000 World Cup sponsored by Cadillac, the Boehm International Challenge Cup, Rolex Gold Cup and Camacho Cup. Crowds of up to 15,000 gather for weekend finals that field such reigning US teams as Whitebirch, Cadillac, Rolex A & K, Boehm, and sleek newcomer Revlon since senior corporate sponsor Cartier late in '87 announced that they could be found "between chukkas" regarding polo, at least in the US.

In private boxes and public spaces overlooking the International Field, weekend throngs mingle with Palm Beach beauties who have seen everything, Hollywood troopers whom everyone has seen and seen, and fresh-faced preppies chomping hotdogs and swilling beer – and also Pimm's Cups. At fieldside, tailgaters have ideal vistas of pre-game spectacles that range from a brace of comparisoned elephants to a gleaming cavalcade of antique coaches or a demonstration of Thoroughbred show jumpers on anti-gravity gallops over a set of Olympic hurdles.

It's all horsey catnip to polo cognoscenti such as Yves Piaget, elegant Mollie Wilmot, 10-goalers Ernesto Trotz with Alfonso and Gonzalo Pieres, C.Z.Guest, the Rajmata of Jaipur, polo-playing TV star Pamela Sue Martin, author

John Forsythe, Hollywood star Cliff Robertson, "Bluebook" hostess Mary Sanford, hardy playgirl Zsa Zsa Gabor, George Plimpton, Liz Whitney Tippet, Marylou and C.V.Whitney, film star Jane Seymour . . . "the usual crowd, darling."

But for every one of them – because Americans are secret Royalists at heart – the season's ultimate thrill is always a personal and polo-playing visit by Prince Charles, accompanied by his wife the Princess of Wales, still known here as "Lady Di".

Far left WILLIAM YLVISAKER PARADES WITH HIS TEAM, CARLOS AND MEMO GRACIDA AND DALE SMICKLAS. *Above left* JANE SEYMOUR ENJOYS WATCHING HER HUSBAND PLAY POLO. *Above right* PRINCE CHARLES IS INTRODUCED TO GUESTS BY JORIE AND GEOFFREY KENT.

As former chairman of the USPA and founder of the 16-year-old Willow Bend Polo and Hunt Club outside Dallas, affable restaurant industry executive Norman Brinker is cautiously gung-ho about Lexington: "A permament and longterm home for the US Open is very appealing. But the Lexington venue must develop players and teams to support its new programme."

His own development programme has been a resounding success. Today's Willow Bend is a superb 2,600-acre equestrian complex that draws up to 5,000 spectators for major events like the Silver Cup played annually in July. Brinker's home team narrowly lost the '88 Silver Cup to Fort Worth/Upchurch which featured famed 10-goaler Cecil Smith's son Charles who rates a redoubtable 7 goals. Innovative Brinker hospitality features everything from skydivers and Hollywood celebrity teams to post-game symphony concerts and even ballet.

Brinker, who has a talent for freewheeling promotion, recently developed a Willow Bend friendship with the *Dallas* TV star viewers love to hate, Larry (J.R.Ewing) Hagman. "They filmed a show at Willow Bend three years ago," says Brinker. "Hagman fell in love and he's been showing us J.R.'s saintly side ever since. For example, during the '88 Willow Bend Special Olympics charity,

underwritten by local sponsor Corrigan's Jewelers, Larry Hagman as chairman of the ball raised $25,000 for the event's handicapped participants."

Another benefit of Hagman's love affair with polo has been to introduce his TV "wife" Linda Gray to Willow Bend. "When she was honorary chairman of the polo ball," remembers Brinker, "no one stayed home to watch the tube." On-site celebrities of the Hagman-Gray stature, says Brinker, entail a powerful PR asset for such Willow Bend sponsors as Nieman Marcus, Corrigan's and, occasionally, Mercedes.

Above TV STAR LARRY HAGMAN LEADS THE PRE-MATCH PARADE.
Above right GLEN HOLDEN OF THE SANTA BARBARA CLUB JOINS THE CROWD.

The longest line of force – and it is very positive – was drawn for the USPA Lexington event by Glen Holden, director of the Santa Barbara Polo and Racquet Club, who flew in from California for the US Open weekend. To the genial Holden, former governor of the USPA Pacific Coast Circuit, 2-goal player/patron of his Gehache Team and winner of the 1986 Pacific Coast Open, "The USPA established in its own setting and the staging of the Open by the USPA itself is one of the most significant things that's happened to modern polo in the US since Bill Ylvisaker and John Oxley revived Florida polo at PBPCC and Boca Raton. It has to help the sport, even out here in California."

For a large number of Californians in Holden's region, the polo pony now rivals the XKE and the Silver Cloud as preferred weekend transportation. It's not surprising; Santa Barbara riders and drivers are low key, and decidedly upscale. Out there the tarrif is high, the turf beside the blue Pacific is smooth as a billiard table, and there's heady nearly year-round polo weather at sparkling spreads like Santa Barbara Polo and Racquet Club which traditionally hosts the Pacific Coast Open. The special quality of this gem of a club, which dates back to the turn of the century, is guarded closely by insurance magnate Holden and a vigilant board of governors. They are polo purists whose object is to maintain the club's family aura in its flowery fastness between the sea and the lush Santa Inez Mountains, while accepting select polo sponsorships like the Braile Institute. IPF leader Marcos Uranga is a constant visitor, along with high-goalers like Tommy Wayman, Bart Evans, Ruben Gracida and Joel Baker.

As Holden sees it, commercial sponsorship, which the US Open acquired in '88 for the first time ever with Toyota, relieves owners and patrons of expenses that are getting out of hand and even going out of sight. "What's more," he states with coals-to-Newcastle graciousness, "certainly for Santa Barbara Polo Club it has glamorized the sport."

Further south, polo is just as powerful but perhaps more dramatic – even melodramatic – which is just what you'd expect at the highly popular Eldorado Polo Club at Indio California. It sits about 20 miles south of Palm Springs and a mere 20 cinematic heartbeats from Hollywood whose glam poloists, male and female, crowd the annual Uplifters' Cup and a slew of media-hyped charity tournaments, all with close ties to Eldorado's new Bob Hope Cultural Center.

Eldorado was the site of the '87 US Open, an event whose glory was swiftly eclipsed in March, 1988, by what some Californians called "The Rollicking Royal Road

Show," featuring the Duke and Duchess of York. To show what a glimpse of Royals can do even to the hierarchy of polo celebs, in '88 the usual Uplifters' Cup crew of Bill Devane, Doug Sheehan and Alex Cord (a.k.a. Piaget's Chukkers for Charity team), along with showbiz players Tommy Lee Jones and Pamela Sue Martin, were similarly eclipsed, indeed replaced, by a mighty Hollywood "A" team at Eldorado receptions for the Duke and Duchess.

The "A's" sailed with the Royal guests from Walter Annenberg's 208-acre estate to a benefit for the Shakespeare Globe Centre and then a $250-per-plate Cartier luncheon – "A six-figure bash," said then Cartier polo consultant Maggy Scherer. They were real household-name stars like Jack Lemon, Jack Nicholson, Eva Gabor, Armand Hammer (he acts?), Deborah Ruffin, Frank and Barbara Sinatra, Johnny Carson. Oh yes, and also there was a polo game in which the Americans ungallantly defeated the British Guards team 9-8.

As His Royal Highness the Prince of Wales has modestly and also magnificently proven during his 1980s US polo jaunts from Oak Brook to PBPCC and back, when real Royalty meets Hollywood "royalty" on the playing field, the main beneficiary is the Game of Kings itself, thanks to the adrenalin rush of visibility it gets throughout the country. Michael Butler, chairman of Oak Brook Polo Club, Illinois, which is the largest and loveliest US summer polo facility, reports: "We had over 6,000 spectators for the '86 Prince of Wales Cup in which Prince Charles played. He's a true polo superstar; there's no question his presence hypes polo popularity tremendously."

In the late 80s, Royalty – whether bred in England or the glamorous East – seemed to be tracking US polo, and vice versa. It has certainly been true for the new Greenwich Polo Club at Conyers Farm in Greenwich, Conn., established in 1981 by publishing magnate and Thoroughbred investor Peter Brant who is patron and captain of his Greenwich-based White Birch Farms Team. One occasion was Brant's first-ever Americas' Polo Championship held in September '86 on the main field of 1,500-acre Conyers Farm, a luxury polo and private home enclave he envisions as "the Wimbledon of Polo".

At that time Queen Noor of Jordan and the Rajmata of Jaipur joined the social and polo establishments to see a 39-goal Argentine team defeat a 38-goal American foursome 11-10 in the inaugural $100,000 tournament. A crowd of 10,000 roared its approval on that burnished autumn day as Brant's newly created polo drama ended. Special guests like Ivan Lendl, Loretta ("Mash") Swit, Bianca Jagger, Virginia Guest and George Plimpton

purred approvingly as a CBS Sports TV crew taped the awards and went off to post-produce the one-hour special that aired on CBS Sports nationwide was the first time ever US high-goal polo had made it to network television. Not a few of Brant's enthused match sponsors, such as Cadillac, TWA, Rolex, Ralph Lauren, Exrox and Panasonic, rode onto the air with TV commercials to help support this $250,000 show and give US football junkies a fierce, fabulous Sunday afternoon alternative.

Tommy Wayman, whose inspired playing almost rescued that '86 game for his US team, departed saying in his best Texas drawl: "I'd like just one more kiss at the pig," i.e., one more chance at the prize. He didn't get it in the '87 renewal, reborn as the Americas' Cadillac Polo Championship, when the Duke and Duchess of York arrived to watch the Argentines win again 11-8 on a rain-drenched field.

This match was aired over CBS Sports by a determined Peter Brant in association with convinced polo sponsor Cadillac who became title underwriter to what is now the Americas' Cadillac Polo Championship. In 1988 too, for the first time in such a prestigious venue, an official magazine sponsor joined in: the powerful *New York Magazine* which published a colour insert in a pre-game issue with a massive overprint for programme use.

MICHAEL BUTLER OF OAK BROOK CLUB WHOSE ENTREPRENEURIAL SKILLS ARE DOING MUCH TO ENSURE THE CONTINUING DEVELOPMENT OF THE SPORT.

With the example of polo activists like Brant, the Kents, the Ylvisakers and the Scherers, another unique breed of polo loyalists has emerged. They too are activists, successful dreamers. But until they got into polo, and vice versa, we knew them mainly as the characters they played on screen. In polo, Hollywood's healthiest addiction, the only roles they play are themselves – vividly, a bit violently, and very glamorously. There are no SAG benefits for these new authentic role players, and payment consists of an airline ticket to the tournament they'll play. They couldn't be happier with the arrangements.

Of the new polo addicts, best known are Piaget's Chukkers for Charity team Alex Cord, archangel in the TV series *Airwolf*, along with Doug Sheehan and Bill Devane of *Knots Landing*. They're often joined by Jameson Parker of *Simon and Simon* and Pamela Sue Martin of *Dynasty* fame. Theirs is actors' equitation of a high degree in the Piaget polo/altruism programme that began in 1986 when, as Piaget President Jerry Grinberg says, "We struck a deal under a tree at Meadowbrook, L.I."

Suffering for their sport, perhaps, more gladly than their art, these willing stars of Babylon at PBPCC in their annual appearances dismount from polo ponies to mount charity podiums. Between 1985 and 1987, for example, they have helped sponsor Piaget raise nearly $400,000 for St. Mary's Hospital of West Palm Beach in conjunction with Piaget's then-sponsored $100,000 World Cup.

Why do they play? There are inner goals as well. Actor and novelist Alex Cord, who played for Piaget at a Shearson Lehmann '85 tournament at Old Westbury Gardens on Long Island, on the still active Meadow Brook grounds, says a subsequent charity promotion of himself holding the March of Dimes Poster Girl in his arms "is a picture of the happiest moment in my life". Cord himself, who saw his first polo match at Meadow Brook as a child on crutches, conquered polo at age 11.

Movie stars in polo saddles have been around since Jack Oakie and Mary Brian shone in Paramount's 1930 polo film *The Social Lion*, and Hollywood greats like Darryl Zanuck, Leslie Howard, Spencer Tracy and Will Rogers played at the old Uplifters' Club. But there's a real schtick-and-ball resurgence in the entertainment industry, particularly in California. Mallet-wielding celebrities are increasingly seen not only in Eldorado but in the six-year-old $15 million Griffith Equestrian Center which houses Los Angeles' gift to arena polo the Equidome with seating for over 4,000 spectators. Brainchild of Al Garcia, the Equidome's four-chukka polo arena, which fields top international high-goalers on its tanbark surface, is also a carnival where the media find great copy in the spectator crowds. Among the horsey glitterati these days are Sly Stallone, Stefanie Powers and Robert Wagner of *Hart to Hart*, Stacey Keach and actress Dorrie Forstmann, a relative newcomer who sponsors here own polo team called Risky Business – for obvious reasons.

Left LONG-TIME ENTHUSIAST STEPHANIE POWERS WITH THE MEXICAN PROFESSIONAL ANTONIO HERRERA.

Though not yet as dear to the hearts of moviemakers as to movie "players", there are encouraging cinematic signs for the Game of Kings. In 1988, Santa Barbara's Glen Holden, who is an arena polo *aficionado*, took time out from his Pacific Coast Circuit chores to organise funding for a brand-new TV show called *Power Polo*. It was produced in Los Angeles for worldwide distribution in 1988-89, says Holden, with the goal of expanding international interest in the sport, particularly among youngsters who can literally play with just one horse in their local arenas.

The seminal polo movie of the 1980s remains the Rolex-sponsored *World of Polo*, produced, written and directed by David Michaels of Trans World International for Rolex in 1980. The original 90-minute movie is a stunning and lyrical work ranging from polo's Central Asian origins to the dash and drama of today's high-goal tournaments in polo centres from Europe and the US to Argentina. Unfortunately, *World of Polo* has never had a network audience, save in shortened form for regional network

affiliates. But in this era of buccaneer taping the show has found its way into most of the world's major polo clubs. And the polo community is grateful indeed.

Since the early 1980s, US network sports and lifestyle programmers have increasingly covered segments of major tournaments throughout the US, concentrating on south Florida, Texas, California and NY/New England. Major sponsors, such as Cadillac, Rolex, Boehm and Rolls-Royce, have all underwritten one- and two-hour sports documentaries of their prize events, marketed their quota of TV spots and aired these shows nationwide on leading cable networks like USA and ESPN. Greenwich Polo Club alone, through the efforts of owner Peter Brant, annually airs high-goal polo for a network audience on CBS Sports.

Above PETER BRANT, A HIGHLY SUCCESSFUL AND OCCASIONALLY CONTROVERSIAL MEMBER OF THE INTERNATIONAL POLO COMMUNITY.

Strong underpinning of polo's TV and film presence is the selective yet steady growth of corporate support. Why the seemly haste today among blue-chip and mid-level companies to sign up teams and tournaments?

It is a question of image. Elusive as a polo ball trimming the turf at 100 mph is that quintessential prize – the perfect corporate image. As polo comes thundering back on to sports pages, fashion layouts and TV screens, astute sponsors discern in the gruelling glory of the game and the worldly aura of its players and fans a metaphor of their own mystique, and a made-to-order marketing tool. Just as seductive to corporate decision-makers as polo's dash and class are its still uncluttered prospects for image bonding.

Who are these fortunate folks? National and international manufacturers of patrician specialties, are not a few commodity makers that together entail some 200 companies who yearly spend nearly $7 million on US polo sponsorships. In the late 1980s a select survey of major polo sponsors finds some surprising newcomers, some classic dropouts, some realignments and overall a growing confidence in brand-name identification with the quality inherent in polo's elegant strife. Its prize is the perception of the aware consumer, especially that third of all US polo spectators who have household incomes exceeding

$150,000 and the quarter who own at least $1 million in securities.

"Elegance, quality, the Thoroughbred look," says Toyota's PR manager Ed Snyder; "these are the marketing elements we identified with when Toyota decided to become title sponsor of the US Open at Lexington." It was a first for both sides. Until 1988, the prestigious tournament had never had commercial sponsorship, nor had Toyota considered polo. Another innovation at the '88 Open was dual team and event sponsorship by Coca-Cola, first for longtime event sponsor Coke. Their new programme is planned to be hyped nationwide by a Coke/polo TV and print advertising campaign which will inform millions that polo is one of the things that go better with Coke. You couldn't pray for vaster promotional reach. Egalitarian? And how, and why not says Allan Scherer, who likes to call such marketing windfalls "extended media reach".

People like Margaret Scherer and her peers from PBPCC and Greenwich to Dallas and Eldorado have redesigned corporate sponsorship to suit the Game of Kings so that corporate kingpins are taking notice. Today's surge in polo sponsorship throughout the US is remarkable when a decade ago the sum total of corporate support probably would not have kept one top club's high-goal schedule

going for a full season.

The crucible of corporate sponsorship as it is known today was Palm Beach Polo and Country Club, unofficial, and undisputed, world capital of polo. As structured by its founder Bill Ylvisaker, with associates like Maggy and Allan Scherer, PBPCC in the 1970s was where grandiose, newly created tournaments like the $100,000 Piaget World Cup, the Rolex Gold Cup and the Cartier Challenge Cup were shaped and marketed, principally to corporations wooing the very rich – upscale markets say Madison Avenue wordsmiths – whose crests then began appearing on the International Field, on team jerseys and in vigorous brand-name national and international promotions.

Their names are legend; their polo fans, and polo friends, are legion. Consider Cadillac, Revlon, Coca-Cola, Piper Heidsieck, Boehm Porcelain, Piaget, Pimm's, Michelob, Ralph Lauren, Cartier, BMW, Fiat, Lancel. Most of them are still on board in one guise or another. Some, like Cartier, are "between Chukkars" in the US, though not abroad. You can spot the emblems of these polo pioneers as they move north and west with the high-goal seasons from Palm Beach and Boca Raton to Greenwich, Saratoga and Myopia and then Oak Brook, Willow Bend, Santa Barbara and Eldorado. And there are scores of high- and medium-goal centres in between where the same corporate flags fly.

Their involvement is the lifeblood of modern polo. USPA past president Don Little says: "Sponsor use of top-end polo helps publicize the sport, enhance growth, encourage young players. Those benefits must filter down to polo's grass roots where our future lies." And Ylvisaker: "There's no question corporate support has given the game a terrific leg up. And for the sponsors there's an aura, a visibility in the product/polo association as unique as it is hard to measure. But the benefit is there or they wouldn't keep coming back."

Above THE COCA-COLA INTERNATIONAL TEAM: SKEETER JOHNSON III, MARCOS HEGUY, ERNESTO ASTRADA AND JEFF ATKINSON. ***Far left*** TOYOTA'S PUBLIC RELATIONS TEAM ARE ON HAND TO MAKE THE BEST OF THEIR SPONSORSHIP. ***Above left*** MAGGY SCHERER WITH LEVERETT MILLER, ARCHITECTURAL CONSULTANT AND FOUNDING MEMBER OF THE POLO MUSEUM.

For each sponsor dropout at PBPCC these days, there's another waiting for a crack at his own splendour on the grass before the fans on field number one. And then there's another kingly quirk about polo that encourages corporate entrepreneurs. They can see some of their own right down there on the field scoring goals and company kudos, and often making fortune: Bill Ylvisaker himself, White Birch captain Peter Brant who founded Greenwich Polo Club, and Les Diables Bleus owner and French art investor Guy Wildenstein, to name a few of polo's patrons.

The game of corporate sponsorship is hardball all the way, just as polo itself, whose $3\frac{1}{4}$-inch willow root sphere flies at 100 mph from a well-aimed mallet is probably the hardest of all hardball games. Consider the figures for luxury backers with limited budgets. Sponsorship costs, depending on depth of tournament involvement, generally range from $50,000 to $250,000. Team sponsorship for a glamour foursome and their mounts may soar from $250,000 to $500,000 annually. For the timid corporate comptroller, however, Ylvisaker at PBPCC had a ravishing role model. In 1983 after Cadillac's first full season as Official Car of Palm Beach Polo, their sales in Palm Beach County nearly doubled within two months. Now there is aura with action.

For the third successive year in '88, Cadillac sponsored the Americas' Polo Championship at Greenwich Polo Club in Conyers Farm, Conn., where the Argentines continued their unbroken dominance over the US. Meanwhile, at PBPCC in '87, Cadillac had already secured its "official car" eminence and also opted for title sponsorship of the $100,000 World Cup as Piaget took time out. The polo-loving motor car company that year also introduced its Cadillac Polo Team based at PBPCC, featuring the 10-goal brothers Carlos and Memo Gracida. In 1987, Cadillac went west to become sponsor of the American League at the Los Angeles Equestrian Center. Says company ad director Peter Leven "Cadillac's polo/marketing report card for the past five years has been a string of straight As. Cadillac is very pleased to ascend to the top of the polo world."

A gentler slope is preferred by Pimm's. Pimm's of the lovely hue and the secret stuff, in for the long haul. Pimm's organises a series of scheduled "Pimm's Days" at scores of polo clubs. These occasions may range from a low-goal Pimm's match to a costumed tailgate competition complete with picnic and Pimm's cheer with proceeds usually going to charity. Packing its tropic wallop, Pimm's – a fixture on the US polo circuit since 1975 – goes tailgating after the sun, following the US high-goal season

from Boca Raton and PBPCC in Florida to Atlanta's Vinings Polo Club, Harrah's in New Jersey and Greenwich and Saratoga in the northeast, then westward ho to Napierville and Oak Brook near Chicago and on to Santa Barbara and Eldorado in the land of the navel orange whose fruit, some say, is occasionally used in Pimm's No. 1 Cup. The Pimm's display and serving wagon, so familiar to US polo fans, creates a genteel presence, a way to celebrate a polo victory or round out a weekend tailgate gathering with a festive libation.

Irrepressible Helen Boehm has been a persuasive corporate player on the high-goal circuit for nearly a decade. With guts, glitz and lots of long green she has brilliantly used her polo sponsorships to merchandise her prestigious Boehm Porcelain collections from the US to England and Western Europe including, says Helen, the Vatican. Even the Pope must have been impressed no less by the quality of Boehm porcelain than by her high-goal foursomes which are known for fielding Argentine supernovas like Gonzalo Tanoira and Ernesto Trotz. Apart from sponsoring her traditional Boehm Cup, an ongoing tournament for Helen is her $40,000 Boehm International Challenge Cup for young players age 18 to 27. The match is held annually in memory of young Billy (William W.) Ylvisaker. "We are seeing here the future 8-, 9- and 10-goal players of the world," says Helen whose polo passion has generated blizzards of publicity not only for her own endeavours but for the sport of polo in the US and abroad.

Panache beyond price – to match his wonderful timepiece – and altruism without stint, entail the high-goal marketing formula of Piaget president Gedalio Grinberg, whose company was exclusive sponsor of the $100,000 Piaget World Cup from 1983 through 1986. Piaget is doing other things now with its polo time, notably fielding its famed Chukkars for Charity squad from Florida to California. But for connoisseurs of the US polo world, and especially the worldly PBPCC, Piaget represents a trailblazing presence both in sponsored competitions and cause-related events which Piaget uniquely has stressed among corporate peers.

Right JORIE AND GEOFFREY KENT ARE BOTH KNOWLEDGEABLE AND GENEROUS PATRONS OF THE GAME. OFF THE FIELD THEIR PARTIES ARE FAMED.

The results, says Grinberg with good reason, have dramatically enhanced Piaget as well as polo visibility during the sport's 80s period of greatest growth. Grinberg, who developed the renowned Piaget Polo watch in 1975, five years before the company's first high-goal partnership, is the first watchmaker to score high with polo imagery. The effect in brand awareness has been terrific, says Grinberg: "The polo community is the perfect place for us – the image is apt; the market's upscale; the price, for our buyers, is right."

One of the first and surely foremost of modern US polo sponsors is Rolex. The Oyster's their world and all of them are proud of Rolex's famed *World of Polo* film and the seamless bond it dramatises between Rolex and high-goal polo. The Rolex commitment began in 1979 with dual sponsorship of the new Rolex Gold Cup at PBPCC and the Rolex Abercrombie & Kent Team, captained by international high-goaler Geoffrey Kent. Today, Rolex back an extensive tournament and team sponsorship calendar from PBPCC to Greenwich, Oak Brook and points west. Media success derives not only from the highly charged polo centres like PBPCC, but through close working relationships with Geoffrey and Jorie Kent who are also principals of the famed Abercrombie & Kent International adventure safari group. Polo hasn't yet overtaken the sum total of world-class sports and fashion-world advertising and PR at Rolex, but they're neck and neck.

There is, of course, another celebrity. This one is high of heart and fleet of foot, sound of wind and limb, the true master – and sometimes the mistress – of the game. He's given to loyalty and long endurance. His gift is grace under the pressure to excel. He is the polo pony.

Only in the game of polo is an athlete of another species honoured with a "Best Playing Pony Award". And so it should be. The harmony between man and horse may be mythic; on the polo field it is mandatory. Legendary 10-goaler Cecil Smith said it for all time: "The pony is 75 per cent of the game, maybe more. He must have the speed of a racehorse, the quick response of a cow pony, and the timing of a show horse." Experts look for a sensitive mouth, short coupling, deep chest, robust hocks, and that grandest of abstracts – heart.

Top US professional Tommy Wayman knows the pony's worth as well as anyone on or off the field, player or breeder. "A polo pony has to be the greatest animal athlete going," says Wayman, who likes to quote a Texas proverb: "You can cuss my wife and kick my dog, but don't bad-mouth my horse."

The feeling permeates the polo world. Geoffrey Kent tells the story of a recent tournament when he was riding his new mare Fleur in a devastating chukka. There was a bad collision, and then a fall with both rider and Fleur down in a tangle at midfield. Geoffrey's wife Jorie rushed to the scene, knelt down, cradled her husband's head and said: "How's Fleur?"

Left CELEBRITIES, KNOWN FOR THEIR TELEVISION AND FILM APPEARANCES: BILL DEVANE, DOUG SHEEHAN AND ALEX CORD. *Above* THE GREAT CECIL SMITH, WHO MAINTAINED HIS 10-GOAL RATING LONGER THAN ANYONE ELSE IN THE HISTORY OF THE GAME.

Above GEOFFREY KENT'S LOVE OF THE GAME OF POLO TAKES HIM THROUGHOUT THE WORLD. ***Below*** THE KENTS, EVER MINDFUL OF THE NEEDS OF OTHERS, OFTEN USE THEIR INFLUENCE IN THE SPORT TO RAISE MONEY FOR CHARITY.

GEOFFREY AND JORIE KENT

GEOFFREY AND JORIE KENT are a team. As befits the owners of an international travel company they are globetrotters and wherever they are they find a welcome. Generous hosts, they also move in polo's highest circles. Counting HRH The Prince of Wales among their team is certainly a help but then so is Geoffrey's cavalry background and Jorie's polo connections.

Described by *Town and Country* magazine as having been "born with a silver polo mallet in her hand", Mrs Kent's father, Paul Butler, founded the Oak Brook Polo Club, near Chicago, and she married her Kenyan-born husband after meeting him as a player in the Oak Brook club which she was then managing. Both determined winners, their Rolex, Abercrombie & Kent and Windsor Park teams have set a standard of excellence due not only to their players but also to Jorie's continued coaching from the sidelines. She attends most games and can always be seen between chukkas and at half time advising the team members on strategy and tactics. Her able breeding and training programme for their horses also does much to ensure that the teams are rarely far from the winner's circle.

Geoffrey Kent's safari travel firm – plus all his other business interests – can be run from any one of their six homes throughout the world. Each has a communications centre which enables work and play to be carried on in their proper parts. A pioneer of the sponsored team from his own business and through Rolex of Geneva, Kent finds that he can wipe all thoughts of business from his mind when he rides on to the polo field. Remaining on top means that the ability to work hard must be balanced by the ability to play hard.

"My safari world", Geoffrey Kent has said, "is rather like polo – a bit of danger, a bit of excitement, something to get the adrenalin flowing, something that's missing from modern life." He needs a strict fitness routine (a combination of exercises gleaned from Jane Fonda and his time in the British army) to remain in peak condition and this he has to be able to perform anywhere, from a hotel bedroom to an African swamp. In this way Kent ensures that he can take his equal place in the team. Not for him the patronage that requires others to carry him to victory.

THE RESURGENCE OF INTEREST IN ARENA POLO REGULARLY DRAWS CROWDS
OF 4,000 TO THE LOS ANGELES EQUESTRIAN CENTRE.

ARENA POLO

From a peak of popularity in the USA in the twenties and thirties, enthusiasm for arena polo slumped dramatically and it was only kept alive by a few enthusiasts. However, in 1980, America has undergone a considerable revival and is being enjoyed by more and more players who are finding that this version of the game has its own special delights. Play in the arena is a lot quicker than the outdoor variety, with more stopping, turning and changing of direction. Stickwork skills are especially useful and the bold player will always prove the most sought after for the three-person teams.

Played on an area which is ideally some 300 feet by 150 feet (as opposed to outdoor polo which uses an area measuring 300 yards by 160 yards if boarded), arena polo is able to deliver maximum enjoyment value to its spectators. Added to the intimate excitement of the game itself, managements usually provide pre-game amusements and entertainment that considerably enhance the party atmosphere.

Professionals battle for honours in various leagues, team names redolent of their football or baseball equivalents: the Los Angeles Colts, the Fort Worth Argonauts, the Washington Senators, the Dallas Dragoons – and regular spectators support their home side with noisy abandon. The players mostly also enjoy outdoor polo and usually hold a similar handicap for the two games. Notable exceptions are Bradley Scherer (with a 5-goal handicap outdoors and 8-goal indoors), Jo Henderson (6 out, 9 in) and Tom Goodspeed (4 out, 8 in). These differences in handicap reflect, perhaps, the amount of time spent playing in the arena as Goodspeed and Henderson are both mainstays of the Los Angeles Colts.

It is at the Los Angeles Equestrian Centre that the intense and highly charged atmosphere of indoor polo is best experienced. "The Star-Spangled Apex of Arena Polo", as it was dubbed by *Polo* magazine is a relative newcomer to the scene. Since 1982 the 4,000 seat "Equidome", situated in the Griffith Park Equestrian Center near Burbank, has been the showplace of arena polo and the beautiful Angelinos who come to watch it. Media coverage is high and movie people are there in abundance. Sylvester Stallone, Stefanie Powers, Robert Wagner and Stacey Keach are joined by many lesser-knowns watching the four-chukka games which are played with a $4\frac{1}{4}$–$4\frac{1}{2}$ inch inflated ball on a sophisticated tan bark surface.

PAUL WITHERS OF ENGLAND; IN THE HEAT OF THE GAME NOT ALL
PLAYERS AGREE WITH THE UMPIRE'S DECISIONS.

9

POLO ACTION

THE
PIMM'S BOOK OF
POLO

To play and to watch polo is to experience an elemental excitement that is rarely matched in other sports. Whatever the intricacies of the rules, the first-time spectator cannot help but thrill to the bold sights and sounds of two teams in intimate and concentrated combat.

In polo the love and trust between horse and rider reaches its apotheosis. One serves the other, and there is no finer sight than the almost Centaur-like man and horse as one. With a singularity of purpose the galloping player reaches after the small white ball. Fellow mounted players dash on in front or push in at speed. The game is all at this moment.

This is a game for individual stars, for brilliant horses, men and women, but it is also a team game which requires pace and technique. Skills of horsemanship are highly rated, hand-eye co-ordination is essential for the hitting of the ball, courage and fearlessness are highly prized – all fitting into a long-established scheme of things that seems to obay some basic and inalienable law of nature.

Polo offers in one place what must often be searched out in many elsewhere. The speed of the racetrack; the hard contact of rugby or American football; the drama of tennis; the team tactical skill of cricket; the intellectual challenge of chess; and the elegance and finesse of the smartest of parties.

As an understanding of the more intricate and esoteric aspects of the game increases, nothing of the joy of its exciting experience is lost. The unrivalled pleasure is, in fact, enhanced. The fundamental 'thrill' remains, but seeing and recognising a brilliant strategic move, stickwork which comes from years of practice yet still contains something more, a horse that suddenly seems to slip into another gear, or an 'impossible' pass achieved, is what ensures that those bitten stay under the spell of polo.

The best and most powerful in the world recognise that they cannot conquer polo. This is its special charm. The game is enjoying at present a stronger player vitality, corporate verve and high media visibility than at any time since its Golden Age in the 1930s. Yet when we reflect on these gutsy, gaudy, brilliant times after riding into the 1990s, it is likely that the proudest polo memories will not be of any particular hyped or inflated series of games, but of the human and equine characters on and off the field who played for their own and others' enjoyment. The spirit they display will doubtless continue to live on into the next century. That is polo's legacy of future fame and force.

Above BILL BOND ELLIOTT TRIES TO AVOID CROSSING MIKE AZZARO'S LINE.
Left A DIFFICULT OFF SIDE FOREHAND STROKE IS HOTLY CONTESTED
BY JOHN HORSWELL (LEFT) AND MAJOR WRIGHT.

Above PODGER EL-EFFENDI STRUGGLES TO PUSH GEOFFREY KENT
OFF THE LINE OF THE BALL AND GAIN POSSESSION.
Left *'CHARGE'* — A PASTEL BY PAINTER VIK ADVANI.

10-GOALER MEMO GRACIDA, PERFECTLY BALANCED FOR A NEAR SIDE
BACKHAND STROKE.

OFTEN SEEN AS THE MOST MASCULINE OF SPORTS, POLO IS
NEVERTHELESS INCREASINGLY ATTRACTING WOMEN PARTICIPANTS,
WHO RECEIVE FEW, IF ANY, CONCESSIONS WHEN PLAYING.

Above THE CAVALRY CHARGE OF EIGHT PLAYERS DOWN THE
FIELD IS GUARANTEED TO EXCITE THE BLOOD.
Left PRINCE CHARLES AND HIS TEAM-MATE STUART MACKENZIE
EFFECTIVELY TIE UP JOSE PENA, KEEPING HIM FROM THE BALL OR A
POSITION WHERE HE COULD BE OF USE TO THE OPPOSITION.

Above ALL ATTENTION IS CONCENTRATED ON
THE BALL IN THE FIGHT FOR GOALS.
Left THE LINE-UP FOR A THROW IN BY THE UMPIRE CAN
OFTEN SEEM A MUDDLED AFFAIR BUT MEMBERS OF
THE FRENCH AND BRITISH TEAMS PICTURED HERE CLEARLY
KNOW WHAT THEY ARE DOING.

HITTING A BALL MEASURING NO MORE THAN 3½ INCHES,
WHILST TRAVELLING AT SPEEDS OF UP TO 40 MILES
PER HOUR IS IMMENSELY SKILLED.

AT THE END OF THE DAY THE SATISFACTION OF HAVING
PLAYED WELL ADDS GREATLY TO THE PLEASURE OF
EXPERIENCING AN EXCITING GAME.

THE ANNUAL TOURNAMENT IN ST. MORITZ: THERE IS A NEED TO WRAP
UP WARMLY TO ENJOY THE ACTION BUT IT IS NEVERTHELESS HOT WORK
FOR BOTH HORSE AND RIDER.

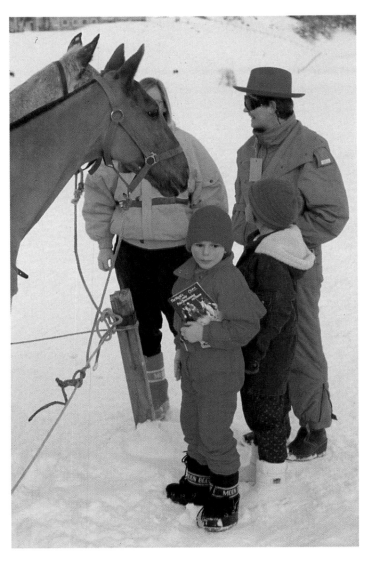

POLO AS PLAYED IN THE CRADLE OF THE MODERN GAME IN GILGAT IN PAKISTAN IS A FAR CRY FROM ITS WESTERN COUNTERPART. WITH LITTLE PROTECTIVE CLOTHING, INJURIES TO THE PLAYERS ARE FREQUENT AND DEATHS ARE NOT UNKNOWN. PERIODS OF PLAY LAST FOR 30 MINUTES AND NO SUBSTITUTION OF MAN OR BEAST IS ALLOWED.

Above DIFFERENT SKILLS ARE OFTEN NEEDED ON THE ICE AT ST. MORITZ. ***Right*** HORSE AND MAN MUST BE BALANCED IF THE SHOT IS TO BE SUCCESSFUL. IN THE BACKGROUND A TEAM-MATE WAITS TO FOLLOW UP THE PLAY AND TO THE RIGHT THE OPPOSITION TRIES TO JUDGE THE BEST MOMENT TO MOVE IN.

THE WINTER SEASON AT ST. MORITZ WITNESSES ONE OF THE MOST
DAZZLING SPECTACLES IN THE POLO CALENDAR AS INTERNATIONAL
TEAMS BATTLE IT OUT ON THE ICE IN SUB-ZERO TEMPERATURES.

MARTIN BROWN DEMONSTRATES THE NEED FOR SUPERB RIDING SKILLS
— COUPLED WITH EXCELLENT HAND-EYE BALL CO-ORDINATION.

MAN AND HORSE AS ONE IS ONE OF THE MOST INTENSE PLEASURES
TO BE EXPERIENCED FOR PLAYER AND SPECTATOR ALIKE DURING
A POLO GAME.

Above ON THE SPECTATOR'S SIDE OF THE FENCE, DAME EDNA
EVERAGE ADDS HER OWN SPECIAL CHARM AT WINDSOR'S PIMM'S CUP FINAL IN 1987.
Left JOHN OXLEY, THE GRAND OLD MAN OF POLO,
TAKES A BREAK BETWEEN CHUKKAS.

ON FIELD THE HORSE IS TRANSFORMED INTO A MACHINE THAT MUST
BE PITTED AGAINST OTHERS. THE FASTER ANIMAL
CAN USUALLY GAIN THE ADVANTAGE.

Above and left ENTHUSIASM RATHER THAN SKILL IS TO THE FORE
IN THE EARLY STAGES OF LEARNING THE GAME, BUT THOSE YOUNG
PEOPLE WHO PERSEVERE CAN SOON IMPROVE AND WILL GAIN A
LIFETIME OF PLEASURE FROM THE SPORT.
Following pages THOSE WHO ENJOY THE NOBLE GAME OF POLO,
BOTH ON AND OFF THE FIELD, EXPERIENCE A COMRADESHIP AND
EXHILARATION THAT IS WITHOUT EQUAL.

GLOSSARY

Arena polo Whilst following the same basic principles, arena polo is played in a considerably smaller space than the outdoor version and requires different strategies. Teams consist of only three players.

Chukka (US spelling **chukker**) Each period of play lasts for seven minutes with up to 30 seconds of overtime. If during that 30 seconds the ball goes out of play for any reason, including a foul, then the umpire signals that the chukka is ended. At the end of seven and a half minutes play stops, in order that players can change their mounts. Matches are of between four and six chukkas and this may be extended if there is a tie between teams.

Equipment Both player and his mount wear safety equipment. High brown boots, knee guards and a helmet are worn by the player who uses a stick or mallet to hit the ball. He may also carry and use spurs and a whip. The pony is equipped with an English-style saddle with an overgirth which helps to stop it from slipping. Leg bandages are compulsory to help protect the lower legs and the tying up of the tail prevents it from becoming entangled in playing strokes. Other tack is found to suit each individual horse and rider.

Field The polo ground is 300 yards long and 200 yards wide, unless boards are used down the side of the field to help keep the ball in play, then it is only 160 yards wide. The goal posts, which are designed to collapse easily on severe impact, are eight yards apart. Penalty lines are marked in white 30, 40 and 60 yards from each back line and the centre of the ground is similarly marked.

Goal When the ball crosses the line at any height between the goal posts, regardless of whether a stick or horse caused it, a goal is scored. Teams change their direction of attack after each goal is scored in order to equalise wind and turf conditions.

Handicap All registered players are handicapped from minus one (in America) or minus two (in Britain) to 10 (the very best). The vast majority of world players are rated at 1 or 2-goal handicaps and 10-goalers are rare indeed.

The handicap represents the player's ability over a six-chukka match and, despite the use of the word 'goal' after the digit, bears no relation to the number of goals he or she might score. The handicap of a team is the sum of the four players' ratings and the side with the lower total receives the difference as a score at the beginning of a match.

Factors considered in awarding handicaps include a player's hitting ability, tactical and game sense, the quality of his horses and horsemanship, team play and sportsmanship.

Hook A player may spoil another's stroke by hooking his stick. For safety reasons this move may only be attempted without reaching over the striking player's mount.

Levels of play Different ruling bodies have different limits for the three main levels of play which are categorised according to the combined team handicap at Low-, Medium- or High-Goal. Local rules also determine upper and lower handicap levels for those allowed to take part in each group and team line-ups might change according to the type of tournament or match.

Line of the ball Having hit the ball, a player is entitled to follow the line of the ball to take a further shot. Opponents may challenge for possession by hooking the player's stick or riding him off the line. The player with the line of the ball might be considered to be on the main road. Anyone coming in from a side road must do so safely or incur a penalty.

Penalties The most common fouls occur when an opponent crosses the 'right of way' created when the ball is being followed on its exact line or closest to it. Most penalties are imposed in order to prevent play which might be considered dangerous to horse or rider. The severity of the foul committed and its place on the field determines the penalty award. This ranges from the giving of a goal to a free hit from the spot where the foul occurred.

Ponies There is no height limit for the horses which play polo but most are between 15 and 15.3 hands high (a hand is four inches). Generally aged between 5 and 15, the ponies are trained to stop and turn quickly and to accelerate well. They must be handy and fearless.

Ponies are changed after every chukka and will usually only play for two periods during an afternoon, with a rest of at least one chukka in between. Polo mounts are still often referred to as ponies, owing to the imposition of a height limit until early this century.

Positions of players Listed as the Number 1, the team forward must be an accurate hitter on fast, handy ponies able quickly to turn defence into attack. He is the main goal scorer.

The Number 2 should devote his time to disrupting the opposition's Number 3 in defence as well as supporting his own Number 1 in attack.

The team's best player takes the Number 3 position and is responsible for controlling the speed and direction of the game, building the play for his forwards.

At back, the Number 4 is in the main defensive position and needs to have a strong backhand. He should be always ready to gallop up from behind, taking loose balls into effective attacking positions.

Referee The referee, or 'third man', sits on the sideline and makes a final decision if the two mounted umpires cannot agree.

Ride-off A player may put his body and his horse against an opponent who has the line of the ball in order to push him off that line and prevent him from striking it.

Spectators Those who attend games as spectators have their part to play and their help in treading the divots thrown up by the horses' hooves is particularly welcomed at half time.

Sticks (US **mallets**) These comprise a bamboo shaft and hard wood head which strikes the ball on the side (not the end as in croquet). The stick *must* be carried in the right hand and varies in length from 48 to 54 inches according to the size of the pony being played.

Time-out The clock is stopped when a penalty occurs or when an accident happens. For safety, a player may call time-out if he experiences broken tack or injury to himself or his horse. Players may change their horses or sticks for any reason at any time but time-out is not allowed.

Umpires Two mounted umpires each cover one side of the field. They can consult each other and impose penalties only if they agree. In the event of a disagreement they confer with the referee on the sidelines.

TEN – GOAL PLAYERS OF ALL TIME

Ten-goal handicap Polo players covet many of life's riches — but most of all they covet the 10-goal handicap rating.

Since the introduction of the handicap system 100 years ago there have been less than 65 10-goal players. Those who have reached the top are superstars, known throughout the polo world for their technical skills with stick and ball, for their superb horsemanship, for their understanding of the game and team play, and for the sportsmanship. They have risen to the dizzy heights through sheer hard work and constant practising, playing year-long and full-time the fastest and most exciting polo imaginable.

There are 13 steps in the handicap ratings, from minus 2 for the absolute beginner to plus 10 at the top. In between there is the world of polo in all its aspects. By far the majority of players are rated below 3 or 4 goals, so the few 10-goalers are justifiably looked upon as the demigods of the game. The select elite who have attained this rating are all men, many of whom came from polo-playing families. English and American players feature strongly in the list but since World War II the South Americans have predominated.

There is no international consensus about handicaps, so it is possible for a man to be a 10-goaler in one country but bear a lower rating in another. At this exalted level, however, the definition is somewhat academic. Ten-goalers chosen by any of the game's national governing bodies will have earned their place in the list.

Foxhall Keene (USA)
Rodolphe L. Agassiz (USA)
John E. Cowdin (USA)
Thomas Hitchcock Sr (USA)
Lawrence (Larry) Waterbury (USA)
J.M. (Monty) Waterbury Jr (USA)
F.W. (Rattle) Barrett (England)
E.W.E. Palmes (England)
Leslie St C. Cheape (England)
R.G. Ritson (England)
Walter S. Buckmaster (England)
J. Hardress Lloyd (England)
Vivian N. Lockett (England)
Lord (John) Wodehouse (England)
Devereux Milburn (USA)
Harry Payne Whitney (USA)
Louis E. Stoddard (USA)
J. Watson Webb (USA)
Luis Lacey (England and Argentina)
Thomas (Tommy) Hitchcock Jr (USA)
Jaswant Singh (India)
Jagindar Singh (India)
Juan A.E. (Johnny) Traill (Argentina)
C.T.I. (Pat) Roark (England)
J. Malcolm Stevenson (USA)
W. Hopping (USA)
Elmer J. Boeseke (USA)
Cecil Smith (USA)
Stewart B. Iglehart (USA)

Michael G. (Mike) Phipps (USA)
Gerald Balding (England)
Enrique Alberdi (Argentina)
Luis Duggan (Argentina)
Carlos Menditeguy (Argentina)
Juan Carlos Alberdi (Argentina)
Julio Menditeguy (Argentina)
Robert (Bob) Skene (USA)
Roberto Cavanagh (Argentina)
Juan Carlos Harriott (Argentina)
Francisco E. Dorignac (Argentina)
Gastòn R. Dorignac (Argentina)
Horacio Heguy (Argentina)
Gonzalo Tanoira (Argentina)
Sinclair Hill (Australia)
Daniele Gonzales (Argentina)
Alfredo Harriott (Argentina)
Alberto Pedro Heguy (Argentina)
Eduardo Moore (Argentina)
Gonzalo Pieres (Argentina)
Alfonso Pieres (Argentina)
Ernesto Trotz (Argentina)
Christian La Prida (Argentina)
Juan Carlos Otamende (Brazil)
Thomas Wayman (USA)
Guillermo (Memo) Gracida Jr (Mexico)
Carlos Gracida (Mexico)
Marcos Heguy (Argentina)

INDEX

PICTURE CREDITS

Vik Advani   202

Terry Allen   46 top, 70, 80 top, 85 top right and bottom, 95 top, 96 right, 156 bottom

BBC Hulton Picture Library   46

BBC Hulton Picture Library/Bettman Archive   32, 35 bottom

Ross A. Benson/Los Angeles Equestrian Centre   196

British Library   19, 20, 21 top

Paul Brown   10

Eskenazy Oriental Arts   16

F. Faggiani/Polo International   68, 88 bottom, 123, 139

Lady Edith Foxwell   30 right

Granger Collection   29

Philip Iglehart/Museum of Polo and Hall of Fame   21 bottom, 40, 43 bottom, 53, 30 left, 125 top

Keystone Collection   23, 35 top, 42, 44, 45, 46, 48, 50, 64, 114, 115, 124

Kobal Collection   87 bottom left

Xavier Lecoultre   14-15, 148, 149, 216-7

John Lloyd   18, 24, 122

David and Janette Lominska   Cover, 2, 4-5, 60, 63, 74, 76, 78-9, 80 bottom, 82, 87 top and bottom right, 91, 92, 93, 94, 95 bottom right, 97 bottom left and right, 98, 109, 123, 129, 138, 141, 142, 147, 152, 159, 160, 161, 165, 168, 171 top, 172, 174, 180, 181, 182, 185, 186, 187, 193, 194 bottom, 198, 203, 206, 209, 212, 213, 219, 222-223, 226, 228, 232-233, back flap

National Archives   26

Peter Newark's Western Americana and Historical Pictures   22, 132

Christine Nys   1, 8

Palm Beach Polo and Country Club   86

H.M. The Rajmata of Jaipur   33, 56, 58, 112

Mike Roberts   49, 51, 57 top, 62, 66, 71, 75, 84, 85 top left, 88 top, 95 bottom left, 96 left, 97 top left, 99, 100, 102, 104, 105 top left and right, 106, 108, 116, 117, 118, 119, 120, 121, 127, 128, 130, 133, 137, 143, 144, 146, 153, 154, 155, 156 top, 157 top left, 157 top right, 157 bottom, 162, 163, 170, 171 bottom, 194 top, 200, 201, 204, 205, 207, 208, 210, 211, 214-215, 218, 220-221, 227, 230, 231

Frank Rohr   54, 57 bottom, 176, 177, 178, 179, 183, 188, 189, 191, 192

'Snoopy'/Ricardo Motran   72, 73, 89, 110, 134-135, 145, 150, 166, 167, 225, 229

The United States Polo Association   39, 43 top, 58, 31, 90

Bob Vickers/Fotocall   6-7

Vanity Fair   28

Victoria and Albert Museum   12

Max Whitaker/Impact Photos   65, 69, 101, 125 bottom

Jack and Marjorie Williams   77, 126, 140

Mackenzie Publishing Ltd and Stanley Paul & Co Ltd have made every effort to acknowledge every agency or photographer whose work has been used in this book